# Macroeconomic Dynamics

# Macroeconomic Dynamics

*A Marshallian Synthesis*

Hugh Rose

Basil Blackwell

Copyright © Hugh Rose 1990

First published 1990

Basil Blackwell, Inc.
3 Cambridge Center
Cambridge, Massachusetts 02142, USA

Basil Blackwell Ltd
108 Cowley Road, Oxford, OX4 1JF, UK

*Library of Congress Cataloging in Publication Data*

Rose. Hugh, 1920–
      Macroeconomic dynamics : a Marshallian synthesis.
          p.     cm.
      Includes bibliographical references.
      ISBN 1-55786-037-8
      1. Macroeconomics.   2. Statics and dynamics (Social sciences)
3. Neoclassical school of economics.   I. Title.
      HB172.5.R67 1990
      339--dc20                                         90-113
                                                          CIP


*British Library Cataloguing in Publication Data*
A CIP catalogue record for this book is available from the British Library.

Typeset in Times on 11/13 pt
by Colset Private Limited, Singapore
Printed in Great Britain by Billing & Sons Ltd., Worcester

# Contents

# Preface

This book has grown out of my lectures to graduate students over many years, at the University of Toronto from 1963 to 1965, at the University of Rochester from 1965 to 1969, and at the Johns Hopkins University since 1970. Many of the components for a general macrodynamic framework are to be found in my paper "Effective demand in the long run" (Rose, 1973), delivered in 1970 at the International Economic Association's Jerusalem conference on growth models. Missing, however, at that time was the crucial idea, contained in my piece on Say's law published in the *Journal of Macroeconomics* (Rose, 1985), of linking with these dynamic components the Marshallian temporary equilibrium forged by Keynes and some of his Swedish contemporaries. A highly condensed version of the book appeared as an article entitled "Aggregate demand and supply analysis" in *The New Palgrave* (Rose, 1987).

I wish to express my gratitude to Masahiro Kawai and Louis Maccini for a constant stream of stimulating discussions over the years: to David Bizer and Stephen Blough for helping me towards an understanding of the "new classical" macroeconomics; and to Carl Christ, Masahiro Kawai, Louis Maccini, Peter Newman, Michael Ormiston, James Tobin and Alan Walters for their comments on the manuscript while it was being written.

Hugh Rose

# Acknowledgements

Thanks are due to the Royal Economic Society and the Macmillan Press Limited, London and Basingstoke, and to Cambridge University Press, Cambridge, holders of the World rights (excluding North America) and of the North American rights respectively, for their permissions to quote extensively from *The General Theory of Employment, Interest and Money* by J.M. Keynes (London, 1936); from *The Collected Writings of John Maynard Keynes*, volume XIII edited by D. Moggridge (London 1973); and from *Employment and Equilibrium* by A.C. Pigou (London, 1941).

# Introduction

Whenever in a group of theories each member can be represented as a special case of a more general system, a deeper understanding can be obtained, both of the theories themselves and of their relationships to one another, than would be possible if they were merely laid side by side for inspection. This remains true even if the general system fails to preserve exactly the models originally fashioned to express those theories.

In this book such a general system is constructed and put to use as a unifying framework for theories of macroeconomic dynamics. Its immediate concern is with the traditional "disequilibrium" macrodynamics – with theories that typically admit unfulfilled expectations or imperfectly functioning markets as dynamic determinants. But the assumptions of perfect foresight and the universal clearing of markets will also be accommodated. My own limitations force me to confine the theories under consideration to those which are concerned with a closed economy. While I shall pay attention mainly to formal relationships, I shall also attempt to place the theories in the history of economic thought, and in particular to demonstrate the significance and continuing relevance of some heated past controversies.

The object of this introductory chapter is to clarify my approach to this undertaking, and to explain why I call it a Marshallian synthesis.

## 1 Period Analysis

There are two ways of treating the time factor in economic dynamics. On the one hand there is period analysis. An elementary period is postulated, which can (but need not) be arbitrarily short.

We shall call it an *instant*. It is "the minimum effective unit of economic time" (Keynes, 1936, p. 47n). A distinction is made between the parameters of an instant and its events. The parameters are given or determined at the outset of an instant and change only from one instant to the next. They consist of its data, functions of the data and of its events, and variables determined at the outset by the data, the functions, and behavior assumptions. The events are variables determined during the instant by the parameters and by behavior assumptions. If there is interconnection between the parameters or the events of one instant and those of another, their motions will be solutions either to a system of difference equations or, if the length of the instant tends to zero, to a system of differential equations.

On the other hand there is point-of-time analysis. It is assumed that variables change only at discrete points on the time axis. Nothing of consequence happens between two successive points of time. If there is interconnection between their values at different points of time, a sequence of their magnitudes will be a solution to a system of difference equations.

In economic dynamics point-of-time analysis is usually inferior. For, in the first place, a system of difference equations such as

$$\frac{\mathbf{x}(t+h)-\mathbf{x}(t)}{h}=\mathbf{f}[\mathbf{x}(t),t;h]$$

may have solutions which would not occur if the interval $h$ separating successive magnitudes were sufficiently short. Since in economics there is rarely a natural interval separating successive magnitudes of all the significant variables, such solutions should usually be excluded as artificial; "cobweb" theories of agricultural cycles, for example, clearly suffer from this defect, inasmuch as they assume that no significant information accrues between harvesting this year's crop and planting for next year's. This is not an argument for rejecting the use of difference equations. Some theories are much more simply expressed by them. But it is an argument against adopting as normal a procedure that rules out passage to continuous time by assumption.

Secondly, but more importantly, in point-of-time analysis the distinction between events and parametric variables becomes a distinction between those variables that are and those that are not determined at each point of time, whereas in period analysis, while events are determined inside the instant, there may be some parameters that are determined at its outset.

I have chosen to formulate the dynamics in terms of period analysis mainly in order to exploit this second aspect of it.

## 2 Temporary Equilibrium

I propose to employ the "method" of (Walrasian) temporary equilibrium. It is defined by the assumptions (1) that in all the markets that open during an instant prices are such that actual demands equal desired demands and actual supplies equal desired supplies (Hicks, 1965, p. 76); and (2) that in this equilibrium of markets the economy moves through time, from one instant to the next, in accordance with dynamic processes governing the behavior of the parameters. This is quite compatible with the idea that there may be disequilibrium in a longer-run perspective.

Clearly many different concepts of temporary equilibrium are consistent with the above definition, distinguished by their specification of the items listed as parameters. Among them, however, only three have achieved general acceptability. For convenience they will be called here the Hicksian, the classical, and the Marshallian neoclassical concepts.

In *Value and Capital* (1939, p. 122) Hicks asserts that there will nearly always be some goods whose production can be changed within the instant. Applying this principle to macroeconomics in his famous article (Hicks, 1937) on the *General Theory* (Keynes, 1936) he treated labor as a perfectly variable factor for the individual entrepreneur, thereby claiming the full-employment counterpart to the *IS–LM* equilibrium as the economy's temporary macroeconomic equilibrium. Not only money income and interest rates but also employment and output are determined by the clearing of markets within the instant, given the parametric stock of capital etc. This still seems to be the prevailing concept of temporary equilibrium in macroeconomics. A difference between planned investment and planned saving is usually taken to indicate a net excess demand for final output.

But there is a grave difficulty attached to interpreting the situation as an equilibrium when there is an excess supply of labor. By Walras' law the values of the excess demands for all items traded within the instant must sum to zero, if abstraction is made from transfers. How can there be an excess supply of labor with no excess demand for anything else?

One way of solving the problem is to call upon the ingenious distinction drawn by Clower (1965) and Patinkin (1965, ch. XIII) between notional and effective excess demands, in order to claim that the effective excess supply of labor is zero even when the notional excess supply is positive: the unemployed are constrained by "the *force majeur* of insufficient demand in the commodity market," and therefore also in the labor market (Patinkin, 1965, p. 322, and p. 333, footnote 22) from exerting any pressure in other markets. The economy moves in a *non-Walrasian* temporary equilibrium, in which the clearing of markets is subject to quantity constraints. For a survey of this approach see Drazen (1980).

One might be tempted to conclude that this is the only way, that unemployment due to an excess supply of labor is beyond the scope of the Walrasian temporary-equilibrium method. Such a conclusion is warranted, however, only if we insist on Hicks's assumption that labor is a perfectly variable factor. Indeed, there is a strong case for assuming that labor, like capital, is a quasi-fixed factor for the individual entrepreneur, given or determined parametrically at the outset of each instant. For there are penalties attached to hiring and firing people, and even to varying significantly hours worked, at short notice. But if factor employments are fixed at the outset of an instant their services are not among the items traded within it, so that an excess supply of labor does not imply an excess demand for any of those items, any more than does an excess supply of the services of capital – a situation with which we are quite familiar. The difficulty concerning Walras' law simply does not arise.

This brings us to the classical concept of temporary equilibrium, and to an ancient approach to economic dynamics which, although it arose in the theory of relative prices, turns out to be exceedingly useful in macroeconomics.

In the classical theory of value there was a standard view of the dynamics of prices and production. In the shortest run, market prices are determined in a temporary equilibrium of demand and supply, given each entrepreneur's current employment of the factors of production, and therefore output, but as time passes employments of the factors, and therefore outputs, will be adjusted, under the influence of differences between market prices and current expectations of the costs of production, towards a longer-run equilibrium in which market prices are equal to currently expected marginal costs of production (including monopoly rents). It is implied that entrepreneurs do not possess the gift of perfect foresight; for, if they did, they would have anticipated the currently appropriate factor employments, so that market prices would not deviate from currently expected marginal costs. It is also implied that each entrepreneur is impeded from adjusting immediately any of the factors he employs; for otherwise he could decide the currently appropriate employment of perfectly variable factors after learning current prices. Since expectations are irrelevant to decisions about the employment of perfectly variable factors, the quantities produced would equate the actual marginal variable costs of production to currently realized market prices, as in the Hicksian theory.

The relevance of expectations was explicitly stated by Mill in his *Principles*:

The value at any particular time is the result of supply and demand; and is always that which is necessary to create a market for the existing supply. But unless that value is sufficient to repay the Cost of Production, and to afford, besides, the ordinary expectation of profit, the commodity will not continue to be produced . . . Persons whose capital is already embarked, and cannot be easily extricated, will persevere for a considerable time without profit, and have been known to persevere even at a loss, in hope of better times. But they will not do so indefinitely, or when there is nothing to indicate that times are likely to improve. (Mill, 1871, p. 471)

The classical theorists seem to have assumed that the impediments affect all factors equally; for they distinguished only market prices and "natural" or long-run normal prices. But in the Marshallian neoclassical theory some factors are assumed to be variable in a shorter run than others, in which case decisions about their employment will depend on *short-term* expectations, which we shall formalize as *expectations for the current instant entertained at its outset*, while decisions about the remaining factors will depend on expectations for a longer term. Thus Marshall in his dicussion of normal supply prices says:

Market values are governed by the relation of demand to stocks actually in the market; with more or less reference to "future" supplies, and not without some influence of trade combinations. But the current supply is in itself partly due to the action of producers in the past; and this action has been determined on as the result of a comparison of the prices which they expect to get for their goods with the expenses to which they will be put in producing them. The range of expenses of which they take account depends on whether they are merely considering the extra expenses of certain extra production with their existing plant, or are considering whether to lay down new plant for the purpose. (Marshall, 1920, p. 372)

The importance of the classical dynamic apparatus for macroeconomics lies in the possibility of applying it, or, better still, its Marshallian offshoot, to the theory of changes in the general price level and in aggregate final output. That is what Keynes did in his *Treatise on Money* (Keynes, 1930, chs 9–11) and in the revision of it that he subsequently made.

In the Preface to the *Treatise* (p. v) Keynes writes: "My object has been to find a method which is useful in describing, not merely the characteristics of static equilibrium, but also those of disequilibrium, and to discover the dynamical laws governing the passage of a monetary system from one position of equilibrium to another." His method was to assume that (1) with any given level of real final output the economy moves instantaneously to a temporary equilibrium in which the market for that output and the market for securities are cleared; (2) in such an equilibrium there is in general a difference between the price level of final output and its long-run supply price, implying a net sum of (windfall) profits or losses in terms of money; (3) when the net sum of windfall profits is non-zero it is a force acting on total output and factor employments, the "scale of operations" (p. 125), and on the general price level.

It will be observed that in the *Treatise* Keynes was following the classical writers, for whom the important discrepancy was between market and long-term normal prices. But in the interval between the *Treatise* and the *General Theory* he became dissatisfied with this. The method of the *Treatise* is summarized and criticized in the *General Theory*:

My so-called "fundamental equations" were an instantaneous picture taken on the assumption of a given output. They attempted to show how, assuming the given output, forces could develop which involved a profit-disequilibrium, and thus required a change in the level of output. But the dynamic development, as distinct from the instantaneous picture, was left incomplete and extremely confused. (Keynes, 1936, Preface, p. vii)

Notice that his dissatisfaction was not with the instantaneous picture but with the dynamics it was embedded in. The solution he found consisted in a switch to the Marshallian neoclassical assumption that labor is variable in a shorter run than capital. The employment of labor on a given capital depends on *short-term* expectations. Windfalls are due to the difference between market and short-term normal prices, and cause short-term expectations to be modified.

His change to the Marshallian point of view appears in this passage from the mid-1934 draft of the *General Theory*:

There are, then, two fundamental quantities, if we follow our present line of analysis; namely the expectation of the sale proceeds of the current output of finished goods which leads to the decision to use capital equipment to produce the goods, and the actual value of the sale proceeds which is realised when the goods in question are finished. The former is what matters if we wish to know what determines the volume of employment, and the latter if we wish to know the actual profits of the entrepreneur; though the influences of the two overlap, since production is a continuous process and expectation is gradually modified, largely in the light of the current level of profits. (Keynes, 1973a, p. 424)

The same idea is expressed in chapter 5 of the published version.

Of course Keynes was not alone in this matter. As Ohlin noted in his illuminating article on the Stockholm theory (1937, 1944), a similar idea was behind the Stockholm School's ex-ante and ex-post concepts (1944, p. 89): "In fact Keynes' analysis of expectations in Ch. 5 – which in many ways is similar to the general view in Stockholm – can be regarded as the following up of numerous suggestions in Marshall's 'Principles'."

### 3 The Treatment of Expectations

But there is an objection to the classical and Marshallian neoclassical dynamics which many people today will regard as fatal. It will be said that it depends on a method of dealing with expectations and the unexpected which is not only ancient but antiquated.

That method is as follows. Forecasts are subjective estimates, liable to gradual revision when they deviate persistently from the facts; although one can allow that such deviations need not be the only cause of their revision. Other pieces of information may be relevant. And in some contexts perfect foresight is a convenient assumption, permitting us to simplify a problem without doing great violence to the truth.

The modern way is to postulate that forecasts are conditional expectations of objectively given random variables, so that when there is incomplete information they will be subject to revision in accordance with the calculus of conditional probabilities. In some contexts the additional assumption of "rational expectations" is a justifiable hypothesis, corresponding to perfect foresight in the non-stochastic method. Its great advantage is to allow us to extend the theory of rational conduct both to the use of information and to the process whereby it is acquired. On this account alone it may be that it will eventually supersede the old way, even in macroeconomics.

Nevertheless there is, I believe, a reason why it is not yet able to do so without impoverishing the corpus of macrodynamic theory. Except under the strongest rational-expectations hypothesis – that agents always know the correct model and its parameters – there must always be revisions of expectations in the light of new information, some learning process that must be followed, no matter which of the two strategies one chooses for modelling the unexpected. The trouble with the new method is that as an instrument for deriving optimum learning processes it gives rise to such complexity in the handling of the informational problem that it forces drastic simplification in the economics, and in the way that randomness is introduced into the models. Thus for a program such as mine, involving the integration of theories that do not necessarily assume complete information, the new method is not yet sufficiently developed to be useful.

Perhaps it is just to avoid such ad hoc simplifications that much current research takes the strong hypothesis of rational expectations as an organizing principle in model-building, presumably in the hope that all "interesting" theories can eventually be refashioned under this restriction. All the same I would contend that, since states in which expectations are fulfilled cannot be well defined without reference to the – logically, if not temporally – antecedent states in which they are not fulfilled, the Marshallian neoclassical dynamics would still be the best point of departure for such reformulations.

#### 4 The Plan of the Book

My purpose is to accomplish Keynes's objective in the *Treatise* with the aid of his later Marshallian conception of macrodynamics. I shall construct a set of dynamic equations governing movements of the economy, in a "Marshallian" temporary macroeconomic equilibrium, towards or around a longer-run equilibrium. The dynamics will include revisions of short-term expected (or "short-term normal") prices when the prices of the temporary equilibrium turn out to be different from them, as in Marshall's theory of relative prices. I shall assume constant returns to scale and labor-augmenting technical change, in order that a longer-run equilibrium may be one of steady growth. This system will constitute the unifying framework to which I referred at the start.

The book is divided into three Parts. Part I presents both the temporary equilibrium and the general dynamic equations which move it. Part II deals with theories arising from the assumption that the ratio of the supply of labor, measured in efficiency units, to the stock of capital is a constant. Part III deals with theories in which this ratio is a variable.

#### 5 Aggregative Analysis

I conclude this introduction with an expression of my general approach to aggregative analysis. Keynes laid great emphasis in the *Treatise* on the subject of index numbers. I believe that in principle he was right to do so. For the subject matter of macroeconomics, indeed, one might claim, of any piece of positive economics, is precisely the behavior of index numbers. It is foolish to assume that their components are homogeneous or are in fixed proportions, since index numbers are required just because they are not. For instance, even in the most perfect of actual markets the "law of one price" is a convenient fiction. The actual price recorded will be some kind of average, sometimes accompanied by a measure of dispersion. In macroeconomics the indices of chief importance are highly aggregative: final output, employment, the stock of capital, the general level of interest rates, the general price level, etc. My purpose in what follows will be served at this "highest" level of aggregation.

The idea, that there exists a fundamental non-aggregative system with which the relevant set of indices should be consistent, is one from which I strongly dissent. The decision to be made is always how far to disaggregate, never how to justify departures from this imaginary construct. If it were not so, we should be in a position to specify, for example, the true number of commodities in the US economy. Obviously we are not.

The index numbers are taken to reflect the average behavior and experience of economic agents. Deviations from the average other than those predicted by a model could not be inferred from it even if everyone knew it in detail. Nevertheless they occur, and lack of knowledge concerning their whereabouts is one of the reasons why windfall profits and windfall losses, like unemployment and unfilled vacancies, can persist.

# PART I

A "Marshallian" Temporary Macroeconomic Equilibrium: Statics and Dynamics

# 1

# A Model of Temporary Equilibrium

## 1.1 Preliminaries

### The Formation of Prices

We shall allow the length of the instant to tend to zero, in order to use differential equations for the processes governing the movements of the parameters. Nevertheless it is necessary to be explicit about the order in which events are assumed to occur in it.

The assumption of market clearing is a decision to evade the intractable problems created by false trading (trading at disequilibrium prices). To this end we shall adopt a device used by Hicks (1939, ch. IX). Prices are constant during the instant (p. 122). The excess-demand functions give us the net excess demands at any particular set of prices, if those prices are fixed at the start and adhered to throughout the instant (p. 128). But the higgling of the market establishes the temporary equilibrium so rapidly that equilibrium prices can be said to rule from the start (p. 123).

In this way we dispense not only with the problem of indeterminacy of equilibrium that arises, in general, when there is a change of prices in the midst of trading, but also with the necessity of distributing in some way the spillovers that must occur if any market fails to clear immediately.

There is one further assumption about timing that proves to be well worth its cost. Although some time must, in fact, elapse, before the plans that will actually be carried out within the instant at any given set of prices are fully implemented, we can simplify the conditions for the stability of the temporary equilibrium if we define the excess demands that are relevant for the higgling of the market as if all such plans were carried out immediately. In effect, we assume that in the higgling of the market the fact that such plans will very shortly be fulfilled has already been discounted. For otherwise we should have to adjoin to the differential equations for the higgling of the market other differential equations dictating the relative speeds at which those plans were executed, without any strong reason behind their dictates.

### Markets

The temporary equilibrium determines the price level of output as a whole and the general level of interest rates, which must be such as to clear the markets for final output and securities. The term "securities" refers to all instruments of credit other than money. The flow excess supply of securities is by definition the same as the flow excess demand for loanable funds, which will be derived from the flow excess demands for final output and money via Walras' law.

### Money and Banking

We define money as the generally acceptable means of *discharging financial obligations*. There is a central-banking system, and all money is bank-money. The central bank is owned (but not controlled) by the private sector. Thus central-bank-money is "inside" money and there is no "outside" money to augment the community's perceived wealth. *Pace* Metzler (1951) this seems to be a fairly harmless postulate. For, even if it is false, outside money will be an argument in the consumption function only to the extent that it is held for future consumption rather than for future liquidity services.

We shall also abstract, for simplicity, from the note issue. There are then two kinds of money: deposits at commercial banks and the reserves of the commercial banks at the central bank. In this chapter we shall assume that the central bank determines total reserves at the outset of each instant, so that the temporary equilibrium will be relative to parametrically fixed reserves.

### The Genesis of Bank Deposits

The genesis of the deposits at commercial banks has been, and perhaps still is, a highly controversial subject. There are two conflicting doctrines, both of which assume that the banks do not collude and that the market for funds, including the market for bank loans, is cleared. One of them, based on the "law of (efflux and) reflux," asserts that the initiative lies with the depositors. Total deposits are regulated by the public's demand for them. The other doctrine, based on the notion of "derivative deposits," asserts that deposits are created by the banks themselves, independently of the public's demand for them. In that case, if the banks do not find it necessary, and are not legally required "to hold any cash reserves but settle inter-bank indebtedness by the transfer of other assets, it is evident that there is no limit to the amount of bank-money which the banks can safely create *provided that they move forward in step*" (Keynes, 1930, p. 26).

It is essential to examine the logical foundations of these alternatives. For it would be difficult to exaggerate the importance of the controversy for the theory of aggregate demand. Moreover, since monetary theory helps to shape monetary praxis, it is also worth while to dwell briefly on its history.

*The Law of Efflux and Reflux in Commercial Banking*    The argument for the law of reflux is as follows. Commercial banks are price makers in regard to their loan rates, and often also in regard to their discount rates for commercial bills. This claim seems to be well supported both by common observation and by the nature of bank loans and bills as contractual agreements, embodying the banks' services as specialists in the market for funds. By monitoring borrowers' activities they are able to provide better terms than non-specialists, who are not in as good a position to protect themselves against default risk. Having chosen optimally their loan rates and discount rates (in competition with the other market rates, of course) they should want to accommodate all creditworthy borrowers, since their specialist activity is their main source of profits. Thus in regard to their loans and bills they are price makers and quantity takers *vis-à-vis* the market as a whole. It follows from this, and from the fact that loans and bills can be repaid at any time, that the public determines the volume of bank loans and bills at rates of interest set by the banks.

If this is granted, net dishoarding of reserves by commercial banks does not in itself bring about a net increase of their deposits; for it does not constitute a net increase of their earning assets. The public is not constrained to accept passively any incipient change of deposits. On the contrary, it can prevent any undesired change of deposits by altering its borrowing from the banks. Futhermore, the public can *determine*, if necessary through the same channel, that the quantity of deposits shall be equal to its demand for them, and has an incentive to do so. For, if an unwanted net shortage of deposits is directed to net sales of securities in the market, there will be a tendency for security prices to move against the net sellers; a tendency that is eliminated if the net shortage is directed to bringing about the desired net increase of deposits.

*Commercial Banks as Creators of Derivative Deposits*   The idea that commercial banks create and destroy derivative deposits, in their attempts to adjust their reserves to the level they desire, has as its logical basis the conception of commercial banks as price takers and quantity makers in regard not only to their portfolio of negotiable securities but also to their loans and bills. Given their current deposits, expected yields, and expected loan and bill rates, they choose the optimum proportion of each asset, including bank loans and bills, to their deposits, while the market determines all actual yields and interest rates in an auction. There must then be a net creation of deposits whenever the banks attempt to adjust their cash reserves, unless a contemporaneous net reduction of total reserves offsets it. For their net dishoarding of reserves brings about a net increase of their earning assets, and so also of their deposits. The public is constrained to accept the net increment of deposits willy nilly, since it has no opportunity to change any of the *quantities* of the banks' earning assets. For a treatment on these lines see Crick (1927, reprinted 1951) and, in more detail, Porter (1961).

I must confess that I do not find this argument at all persuasive. It seems to make no sense for banks to choose the ratio of their loans and bills to their deposits, allowing the market to determine the rates of interest they will obtain, just because they know more than third parties about the particular risks to which their borrowing customers are exposed.

There is also an empirical difficulty. If the initiative for the creation of deposits lies with the banks, a central bank will be able to exert effective control over the supply of deposits only if all commercial banks are member banks, required to hold reserves with it. Otherwise there is a constant danger of expansion by non-members. Yet, in practice, although this requirement is seldom fulfilled, the danger seems not to materialize. Is this not strong circumstantial evidence for the law of reflux, under which no commercial banks have the power to force deposits on an unwilling public?

So far as I can discover, the law of reflux in commercial banking was generally accepted throughout the nineteenth century and in the first two decades of the twentieth. For, although the germ of the doctrine of derivative deposits is sometimes traced to the currency school and their predecessors, in that they are represented as having denied the reflux doctrine of the banking school and theirs, I have not been able to find any hard evidence for this. The opposition of the currency school, in so far as commercial banks were concerned, seems not to have been to the law of reflux per se but to the idea that such banks could avoid insolvency by confining their risky investments to "self-liquidating" real bills, as the banking school believed. On the question of excessive issues, the bullionists and the currency school had in mind the issues of the central bank, not those of the commercial banks.

Thornton, for example, specifically denied in his *Paper Credit* that the note issues of country banks were in themselves inflationary (Thornton, 1939, p. 193): "A third objection commonly made to country banks, is, the influence which their notes are supposed to have in raising the price of articles . . . I propose to prove, that, though a general encrease of paper has this tendency, the objection, when applied to the paper of country banks, is particularly ill founded." Moreover in the course of his argument (p. 207) he draws attention to "the difficulty of finding a channel through which a quantity of paper much larger than common can be sent by the country bank into circulation."

But how about Joplin? In *The Currency Question* (Joplin, 1832, p. 88) we find: "the immediate effect upon prices, so far as they are acted upon by the Currency, must be chiefly caused by the issues of the Country Banks." This appears to be an outright rejection of the law of reflux. However, when he turns to the principle that causes changes in the country banks' issues, "and probably every great fluctuation in prices that has occurred since the first establishment of our Banking system," he says:

The principle in question, which we shall now proceed to consider, is, the effect of the supply and demand for capital upon our Country Bank circulation. When the supply of capital exceeds the demand, it has the effect of compressing it; when the demand is greater than the supply, it has the effect of expanding it again. (p. 101)

The interest of money, when it is abundant, is not reduced; but the circulation, as before observed, is diminished; and, on the contrary, when money is scarce, an enlargement of issues takes place, instead of a rise in the rate of interest. The Country Bankers never vary the interest they charge. (p. 108)

Thus for Joplin the note circulation of the country banks is, after all, determined by the public, not by the banks.

It should be observed that, despite the propensity of the banking school to couple the law of reflux in commercial banking with the real-bills doctrine, the only logical connection between the two principles is that the law requires, and follows from, sound banking practice designed to reduce default risks. What constitutes sound banking practice is a separate question.

The first explicit statement of the derivative-deposit doctrine seems to have been in C. R. Phillips's *Bank Credit* (Phillips, 1920). Schumpeter (1954, p. 1,115) claims that, among others, Newcomb (1885) was a precursor, in that he gave an elementary description of the process by which deposits are created through lending. But in the process Newcomb described (p. 163), there is no suggestion but that the new deposits are willingly held. In fact he provided a clear exposition of the law of reflux (p. 503), which he qualified only by observing that ceilings on interest rates imposed by the usury laws might temporarily disable it by causing an excess demand for bank loans, depriving the public of money it wished to have (p. 511).

Schumpeter also claims that Withers in *The Meaning of Money* (1909, ch. V) espoused the notion that bankers were not middlemen but "manufacturers" of money. Perhaps he is right to find the idea hovering in the air by this time. Nevertheless, when it comes to the point Withers admits that a bank

cannot conduct this manufacture without the assistance of its customers, and it may be contended that these banking credits are manufactured, not by the banks, but by the customers who apply to them, and by the security that the customers bring, and the bankers approve of, as fit collateral. It is certainly true that the banks cannot make advances unless somebody asks for them, and their capacity for doing so thus depends on the needs of the community. (Withers, 1909, p. 72)

It took some time for Phillips's doctrine to become the new orthodoxy, as Schumpeter records (1954, p. 1,114, footnote 5): "It is, moreover, highly significant that, as late as June 1927, there was room for the article of F. W. Crick, 'The Genesis of Bank Deposits' (*Economica*), which explains how bank loans create deposits and repayment to banks annihilates them – in a manner that should have been indeed, but evidently was not even then, 'time-honored theory'." There is, however, a certain ambiguity even in Crick's account of the matter (1951, p. 50). When a banker is short of reserves "he may seek to deter borrowers of all kinds by raising his charges for loans," an admission that is not consistent with the view of banks as price takers in regard to their loans, on which the argument for the derivative-deposit doctrine logically depends.

The same ambiguity occurs in Keynes, who, having expounded the derivative-deposit doctrine in chapter 2 of the *Treatise on Money*, seems to have had second thoughts about it when he came, later in the book, to describing the consequences of a change in central bank reserves. For he says:

Since the injection of an increased quantity of cash (using this word to include Central Bank reserves) into the monetary system will increase the reserve-resources of the member banks, it will, for reasons already explained, render the latter more willing lenders on easier terms; that is to say, the new money stimulates the banks to put resources at the disposal of those borrowers who are ready to employ them, if they are offered on satisfactory terms. (Keynes, 1930, ch. 17, pp. 262–3)

There is no suggestion here, as there was in chapter 2, of the banking system's forcing the public to accept changes in deposits. Perhaps he had by then discovered that Crick's account of the genesis of deposits, to which he had earlier referred with approval for its clarity (p. 25, footnote), was not, after all, free from confusion.

Of course the idea that commercial banks create derivative deposits did eventually prevail. It became the cornerstone of the monetarists' argument for tight control of the money supply. It has directed the approach of twentieth-century economists (and twentieth-century central bankers!) to the problem of aggregate demand and its relation to the business cycle more powerfully than the Keynesian revolution; for it has enjoyed a larger following. The law of reflux disappeared, until the case for it was reopened when Tobin (1963) denied that deposits are, as he vividly put it, "hot-potato" money.

In our model of temporary equilibrium it will be necessary to take account of both doctrines. Enough, however, has been said to justify our accepting the law of reflux as the standard case, while indicating briefly how the model would appear with derivative deposits in a system where all commercial banks are member banks. But the significance of the controversy will not emerge until we address the theory of aggregate demand in Chapter 2.

## 1.2  Temporary Equilibrium with Parametric Reserves

### The Market for Final Output: Aggregate Supply

*Output and Employment*   The flow of final output per unit of capital that will emerge in any instant is given by the production function

$$Y=Kf(N^d/K). \tag{1.1}$$

where $Y$ is an index of real net final output, $K$ is the inherited stock of capital at replacement cost in terms of final output, and $N^d$ is the demand for workers measured in efficiency units.

Let $N^s$ be the supply of workers in efficiency units. $N^d-N^s$ is the excess of vacancies over unemployment. Redundancies are negative vacancies. Firms with vacancies use their workers more intensively while seeking to fill them, so that vacancies do not preclude the production of $Y=Kf(N^d/K)$.

It is assumed for simplicity that there is perfect competition in the market for final output. Let $p$ be an index of final output prices expected for the instant, and $w$ an index of money wage-rates per efficiency unit of labor. At the outset of any instant entrepreneurs choose $N^d/K$ by maximizing the profits per unit of capital that they expect will accrue in it,

$$\max [pf(N^d/K)-wN^d/K]. \tag{1.2}$$

Let $x$ be the value of $N^d/K$ that maximizes (1.2). Necessary and sufficient conditions for an interior maximum are

$$f'(x)=w/p \text{ and } f''(x) < 0. \tag{1.3}$$

Thus the choice of $x$ depends on short-term expectations. Also

$$\max [pf(N^d/K)-wN^d/K]=p[f(x)-xf'(x)]. \tag{1.4}$$

that is, the maximized expected profit deflated by $pK$ is equal to the marginal productivity of capital, and is therefore an increasing function of $x$.

While $p$ is a datum for the instant, we do not at this stage make any assumption about the state of the labor market. Thus it may be either that $w$ is an exogenous datum for the instant or that $w$ is such that the labor market is cleared, so that $w/p=f'(v)$, where

$$v=N^s/K. \tag{1.5}$$

One could use either $x$ or $w/p$ as the parameter for the temporary equilibrium . For the most part we shall find it convenient to use $x$. But in either case the determination of $x$ implies a parametric value of the sum of expected money incomes $pKf(x)$.

*Prices and Windfall Profits*   The sum of actual money incomes, which in a closed economy is the money value of final output, may differ from $pKf(x)$. Let $Q$ be the net sum of unexpected money incomes deflated by $pK$. Thus money incomes deflated by $K$ are $p[f(x)+Q]$. If $\pi$ is the price level of final output, by definition

$$\pi f(x)=p[f(x)+Q]. \tag{1.6}$$

so that $Q$ will turn out to be $\gtreqless 0$ according to whether the market determines $\pi$ to be $\gtreqless p$ within the instant. Since output is a datum for the instant.

$$pQ=(\pi-p)f(x)=[\pi f(x)-wx]-[pf(x)-wx] \tag{1.7}$$

is the net sum of unexpected or *windfall* profits (cf. Keynes, 1930, p. 125) deflated by $K$. In general $pQ$ is a sum of positive and negative terms. In particular $Q=0$ is "perfectly compatible with the profits [sc. windfall profits] of particular entrepreneurs or particular classes of entrepreneurs being positive or negative" (Keynes, 1930, p. 152).

*The Market for Final Output: Aggregate Demand*

*Real Interest Rates and Expected Inflation*   The temporary equilibrium will determine the general level of nominal interest rates. But aggregate demand should depend on *expected current and future real* interest rates, rather than on current nominal rates, which is to say that the relevant variable is an index of current and expected future nominal rates adjusted for expected inflation.

The simplest assumption for expected future nominal rates is that they are equal to current nominal rates, and the simplest assumption for expected inflation is that people expect short-term normal prices to rise indefinitely at a constant percentage rate, which is a parameter for the current instant, although, like the other parameters, it may change from one instant to the next. More precisely, if $\lambda$ is the expected rate of inflation of $p$, if the current instant is $t$, and if $p(s, t)$ with $s \geqslant t$ is the index of final-output prices expected, at $t$, to rule at $s \geqslant t$, then $p(s, t) = p(t)e^{\lambda(t)(s-t)}$. Thus if $i$ is an index of current nominal rates, the general level of real interest rates $r \equiv i - \lambda$ may be (but does not have to be) a good index of expected current and future real rates.

*Planned Consumption*   Since expected future prices are in fixed proportion to expected current prices, we postulate that the money value of planned consumption is positively homogeneous (of the first degree) in currently expected and currently realized prices, $p$ and $\pi$ respectively. Also, since the longer-run equilibrium of many of the theories to be examined is one of constant percentage growth, we shall assume that planned consumption deflated by $pK$ is a function of $Q$ and $x$. It may also depend on the general level of real interest rates $r$. Thus if $C$ is planned consumption deflated by $pK$,

$$C = C(Q, r; x). \tag{1.8}$$

The semicolon preceding $x$ indicates that it is a parameter for the instant. Other parameters can be introduced when they become relevant.

*Planned Saving*   Planned saving is defined as expected income less planned consumption. Thus if $S$ is planned saving deflated by $pK$,

$$S = S(Q, r; x) \equiv f(x) - C(Q, r; x). \tag{1.9}$$

The dependence of $S$ on $x$ represents the influence of $Y/K = f(x)$, and possibly also the influence of the distribution of expected incomes between wages and profits. We shall assume that $S_x$, which ·

has the sign of the marginal propensity to save, is positive. The sign of $S_Q = -C_Q$ is ambiguous. When $\pi$ rises in relation to $p$ with $x$ given, the distribution of $\pi$-deflated *realized* incomes moves against wages-earners, perhaps tending to increase $S$. But this may be outweighed by an intertemporal substitution of present for future consumption when prices are unusually high. It is well known that the sign of $S_r = -C_r$ is also uncertain.

*Planned Investment*   Planned investment is likewise subject to constant returns to scale. If $I$ is the value of planned investment deflated by $pK$, we assume

$$I = I(Q, r; x). \tag{1.10}$$

Additional parameters can be introduced, in order to represent the state of long-term expectations to the extent that it is independent of short-term expectations. $I_x$ is the "marginal inducement to invest." It is non-negative and is zero only if the state of long-term expectations is completely independent of expected short-term profits deflated by $pK$, viz., $f(x) - xf'(x)$. $I_r$ is the effect of the current general level of real interest rates. It is normally negative, but we shall assume that it may be zero, allowing for the "elasticity pessimism" inherent in some of the theories to be considered. A justification for this idea would be that, as we have already noted, $r$ need not be a good index of the expected future real interest rates by which long-term expected prospects are discounted. Finally, since unexpectedly high prices may induce disinvestment in inventories, $I_Q$ is non positive.

   If aggregate money demand deflated by $pK$ is assumed to be $I(Q, r; x) + C(Q, r; x)$, one is including government spending in these terms, thereby adopting the "Ricardo–Barro equivalence hypothesis" (Barro, 1974); for aggregate demand is made to depend neither on taxes nor on the size of the government's debt. From our point of view this is just a convenient approximation, not a matter of principle, which is warranted to the extent that it is an implicit assumption in the theories to be considered.

### Excess Demand and the Adjustment of Prices and Windfalls

The excess demand for final output, deflated by $pK$, is

$$X_g = I + C - f(x) - Q. \tag{1.11}$$

The subscript $g$ is for "goods." After substituting from (1.9) and (1.10) we obtain the excess-demand function

$$X_g = I(Q, r; x) - S(Q, r; x) - Q. \tag{1.12}$$

The price level $\pi$ rises or falls according to whether $X_g$ is positive or negative. So, therefore, does $Q$, so that we may assume

$$\dot{Q} = \epsilon_g X_g \tag{1.13}$$

for the higgling in the market for final output, where $\epsilon_g$ is a positive adjustment coefficient. Therefore

$$\dot{Q} = \epsilon_g [I(Q, r; x) - S(Q, r; x) - Q] \tag{1.14}$$

is one of the two differential equations in $Q$ and $r$ which must be satisfied in the passage to equilibrium.


### The Market for Loanable Funds

*The Flow Excess Demand for Money*    Let $D$ be the aggregate of deposits at commercial banks and $R$ the commercial banks' reserves at the central bank, both deflated by $pK$. The banks' desired ratio of reserves to deposits is $k$. For simplicity it is assumed to be constant. $R$ is a parameter chosen by the central bank at the outset of each instant.

The public's average demand for deposits, also deflated by $pK$, is a function $L(Q, r; x, \lambda)$. The dependence on $Q$ is included for the sake of generality, but $L_Q$ is probably small. There may be a positive income effect on balances desired by capitalists. But, since a portion of bank loans is normally kept on deposit, when a rise in $Q$ reduces the demand for inventories (and correspondingly the demand for bank loans) the borrowers' demand for deposits may also be reduced. On this subject see Keynes (1930, pp. 148-9). The dependence on $r$ and $\lambda$ is normally negative. However, if changes in $r$ induce changes of deposit-rates in the same direction, both $L_r$ and $L_\lambda$ may be small, perhaps even zero. Finally $L_x$ may be negative. For the rise in expected profits with $x$ may increase confidence, reducing the demand for liquidity. (Transactions demand is already largely accounted for by expressing the demand as a ratio to $pK$.)

The law of reflux is assumed to guarantee that the public will have by the end of the instant the deposits it wishes to hold on the average. Consequently, in accordance with the principle stated in the first part of section 1.1 above, the flow excess-demand function for money (deposits and reserves) is defined as if the public's actions to this end were carried out immediately. The commercial banks, however, have reserves that are not, in general, what they need. When their demand for reserves $kD=kL$ differs from $R$ they try to reduce the gap during the instant by *active net hoarding*. Its extent is assumed to be $\beta(kL-R)$, where $\beta$ is a positive adjustment coefficient.

But there may also be *passive* net hoarding. The theory of the precautionary demand for money suggests that, since the terms for unexpected transactions between money and securities at short notice are apt to be worse than those for expected transactions between them, an optimum strategy should require a temporarily passive response to unexpected net receipts, that is, passive net hoarding of them. Now, except in the unlikely event that all goods are bought on credit, unexpected net receipts arise when $Q$ is non-zero. We therefore assume that there is passive net hoarding of windfalls equal to $\alpha Q(0 \leqslant \alpha \leqslant 1)$, where $\alpha$ is a constant.

Passive net hoarding of windfalls is a net addition to the excess flow demand for money. For since it is merely a response to unexpected net receipts in the sale of goods, it cannot be the direct cause of a net inflow of total deposits. The flow excess-demand function for money (deflated by $pK$) is therefore:

$$X_m = \alpha Q + \beta[kL(Q, r; x, \lambda) - R]. \tag{1.15}$$

The subscript m is for "money."


*The Flow Excess Demand for Loanable Funds*    Let $X_f$ be the flow excess demand for loanable funds deflated by $pK$. The subscript f is for "funds." Since it is the flow excess supply of securities, we have

$$X_f = X_g + X_m \tag{1.16}$$

by Walras' law. Thus the excess-demand function for loanable funds is, from (1.12), (1.15), and (1.16),

$$X_f = I(Q, r; x) - S(Q, r; x) - Q + \alpha Q + \beta[kL(Q, r; x, \lambda) - R]. \tag{1.17}$$

*The Adjustment of Interest Rates*   The general level of interest rates $r$ rises or falls according to whether $X_f$ is $\gtreqless$ 0, so that the higgling in this market may be expressed by

$$\dot{r}=\epsilon_f X_f, \tag{1.18}$$

where $\epsilon_f$ is a positive adjustment coefficient. Therefore

$$\dot{r}=\epsilon_f\{I(Q,r;x)-S(Q,r;x)-Q+\alpha Q+\beta[kL(Q,r;x,\lambda)-R]\} \tag{1.19}$$

is the second of the two differential equations in $Q$ and $r$ which must be satisfied in the passage to equilibrium if the law of reflux is valid.[1]

### The Temporary Equilibrium

Passage to a temporary equilibrium must be along a trajectory of the second-order system in $Q$ and $r$ consisting of equations (1.14) and (1.19). An equilibrium is a rest point of this system or, equivalently, a zero of any two of the three excess-demand functions $X_g$ in (1.12), $X_m$ in (1.15), and $X_f$ in (1.17).

*Uniqueness and Asymptotic Stability*   We shall assume that (1) the differential equations are defined for all positive incomes, that is, for all $Q \geqslant -f(x)$, and all positive[2] interest rates $r$, and are continuously differentiable everywhere; (2) an equilibrium exists; and (3) the following inequalities are everywhere satisfied:

$$I_Q-S_Q-1 < 0 \tag{1.20}$$

$$I_r-S_r+\beta kL_r < 0 \tag{1.21}$$

$$\beta k(I_Q-S_Q-1)L_r-(\alpha+\beta kL_Q)(I_r-S_r) > 0. \tag{1.22}$$

In the Appendix to this chapter it is shown that in these circumstances the equilibrium is unique, and is (locally) asymptotically stable regardless of the relative magnitudes of the adjustment speeds, $\epsilon_g$ and $\epsilon_f$.

*The Equations of Equilibrium*   We shall use asterisks to indicate equilibrium values. Putting $X_g=X_m=0$ we obtain $Q^*$ and $r^*$ from the equations

$$Q^* = I(Q^*, r^*; x) - S(Q^*, r^*; x) \tag{1.23}$$

$$\alpha Q^* = \beta[R - kL(Q^*, r^*; x, \lambda)]. \tag{1.24}$$

Then from (1.6) and (1.23) we find that the equilibrium price level is

$$\pi^* = p + pQ^*/f(x) = p + p(I^* - S^*)/f(x). \tag{1.25}$$

Equation (1.23) is Keynes's Fundamental Equation (viii) (1930, p. 128), but with his later definition of $Q$ in terms of short-term expectations, which I referred to in the introduction. The right-hand expression in (1.25) is the form assumed by his expression for the price level of output as a whole in his Fundamental Equation (iv) (p. 137) when $Q$ is so defined.[3] Finally equation (1.24) says that passive net hoarding of receipts from windfall profits is balanced by active net dishoarding of reserves by the banks.[4] Although it is not numbered among Keynes's Fundamental Equations, a special case of it, which we shall shortly state, is implicit in his discussion of the price level of "investments" or "securities" (pp. 140–6).

The meaning of this balance is more easily grasped when it is put into the context of what is happening in the market for loanable funds. Substitution of $Q^* = I^* - S^*$ from (1.23) into the left-hand side of (1.24) yields

$$\alpha[I(Q^*, r^*; x) - S(Q^*, r^*; x)] = \beta[R - kL(Q^*, r^*; x, \lambda)]. \tag{1.26}$$

Since $X_f = X_m$ when $X_g = 0$, this equation expresses the equilibrium in the market for loanable funds when there is equilibrium in the market for final output. It tells us that $\alpha(I^* - S^*)$, which is the portion of $I^* - S^*$ which is not financed by loans from windfall profits, must be financed by funds put into the market by the banks' active dishoarding; and likewise $\alpha(S^* - I^*)$, which is the portion of $S^* - I^*$ which is not matched by borrowing to finance windfall losses, must be matched by funds removed from the market by the banks' active hoarding.

But since passive net hoarding is not a change in the average demand for deposits but a temporary expedient, equation (1.24) must also mean that net windfalls which accrued "yesterday" as passive net hoarding are used "today" to preclude the emergence of any undesired change in the stock of deposits from the commercial banks' active net dishoarding. In effect, the flow of funds accommodating "today's" $\alpha(I-S)$ is "yesterday's" passive net hoarding of windfalls. Thus it is that if there has been no change in the average demand for deposits there will have been no change in the stock of them.[5]

In general $Q^*$ and $r^*$ are jointly determined. There are, however, special assumptions under which the equations have a recursive structure. If the demand for deposits does not depend on interest rates, money incomes and the price level depend only on the condition for equilibrium in the "market" for money, and the condition for equilibrium in the market for goods determines what interest rates must then be. A similarly "classical" result in regard to the determination of money income is implied under the assumption that planned investment is perfectly elastic at a complex of interest rates equal to the short-term average expected rate of profit. For that case the temporary-equilibrium equations have to be changed to

$$I^* = Q^* + S(Q^*, r^*; x) \tag{1.27}$$

$$\alpha Q^* = \beta[R - kL(Q^*, r^*; x, \lambda)] \tag{1.24}$$

$$r^* = f(x) - xf'(x). \tag{1.28}$$

The only value of $r$ consistent with a finite rate of investment is $f(x) - xf'(x)$. At that rate the equality of the flow demand and supply of money determines $Q^*$. Finally, the clearing of the market for goods determines $I^*$ residually as planned saving plus $Q^*$. I shall call this the Tobin–Solow temporary equilibrium. For it seems that its debut was under the auspices of Tobin (1955) and Solow (1956), as a simplifying device in their models of neoclassical dynamics.

At the opposite pole stands the assumption that $I$ and $S$ are functions that do not depend at all on interest rates. Then money income and prices are wholly determined by the equilibrium of the market for output, and interest rates follow recursively from the equilibrium of the "market" for money. Neither monetary policy nor the demand for money affect money incomes or the price level. This has come to be called the "extreme Keynesian" case. But if Keynes was an extreme Keynesian, he was only intermittently so.

### 1.3 The "Liquidity-preference" versus "Loanable-funds" Controversy

There is, however, another assumption which, while it is a special case of our model, Keynes unceasingly regarded as the general case. It is that there is no passive net hoarding of windfalls. From (1.26) it is apparent that the condition for equilibrium in the market for loanable funds depends on whether there is some passive net hoarding or not. If not, $\alpha$ is zero, so that both (1.24) and (1.26) reduce to

$$L(Q^*, r^*; x, \lambda) = R/k. \tag{1.29}$$

The temporary equilibrium requires that both the public and the banks have the money they wish to hold on the average.[6] The net demand for funds represented by $I^* - S^*$ is matched by net loans from windfalls exactly equal to it.

In conjunction with the postulates that $L_r$ is negative and $I_r$ is finite, this is Keynes's "liquidity-preference" theory of interest, according to which the magnitude of $I^* - S^*$ has no direct effect on $r^*$. It affects it only indirectly, in so far as the demand for deposits may depend on $Q$. If $L_Q$ were zero, interest rates would be entirely determined by the equation of the demand for deposits to their supply. But this was not an essential point for Keynes. The essential point was that net windfall profits must (so he believed) create a net supply of loans exactly equal to $I^* - S^*$.

But if $\alpha$ is positive $I^* - S^*$ is not fully matched by net loans from windfalls. Active net dishoarding must fill the gap, viz. $\alpha(I^* - S^*)$, and (except, of course, in the case where $r^* = f(x) - xf'(x)$) passive net hoarding causes $r^*$ to stand above or below the value it would have if $\alpha$ were zero according to whether $I^* - S^*$ is positive or negative. (A proof is given in the Appendix to this chapter.) This is the so-called "loanable-funds" theory of interest, for which see, for example, Robertson (1940, pp. 1-20). Actually the "loanable-funds" theorists' specification of the flow of funds implies that $\alpha = 1$ in equation (1.26). This is inaccurate unless *no* goods are bought on credit. But the important aspect of their theory is that $\alpha$ is positive.

Keynes was to insist on his theory of interest not only in the *Treatise* and immediately after it but also in and after the *General Theory*. His exposition of it in the *Treatise* (1930, pp. 145-6) is clear only up to a point. An excess of $S$ over $I$ does not in itself require a higher "price of new investment-goods" (p. 145) or "price of securities" (p. 146). This conclusion

follows from the fact that [if there is no accompanying change in the demand to hold money or the supply of it] the total value of the investment-goods (new and old) coming onto the market for purchase out of current savings is *always* exactly equal to the amount of such savings and is irrespective of the current output of *new* investment-goods. For if the value of the new investment-goods is less than the volume of current savings, entrepreneurs as a whole must be making losses exactly equal to the difference. These losses, which represent a failure to receive cash up to expectations from sales of current output, must be financed, and the non-receipt of the expected cash receipts must somehow be made good. (Keynes, 1930, p. 145)

But thereafter it lapses into obscurity. The clearest account is in "A rejoinder" (Keynes, 1931):

Next, for my argument, which Mr Robertson contests . . ., that an increase of saving relatively to investment does not in itself bring about any net increase in the amount of purchasing power directed to non-liquid assets. An increase of saving relatively to investment during any period means that the savers find themselves at the end of the period with an increase of wealth, which they can embark at their choice either in liquid or in non-liquid assets, whilst the producers of consumption goods find themselves with an equal decrease of wealth, [obviously the "losses" of the *Treatise* passage] which must cause them to part at their choice either with liquid or with non-liquid assets which they previously possessed. Unless the propensity to hoard of the savers is different from the propensity to hoard of the entrepreneurs – and if it is different, it will mean that there is a change of hoarding propensity for the community as a whole, which change is as likely *a priori* to be in one direction as in the other – it follows that the excess of saving has *in itself*, and apart from its repercussions on the aggregate propensity to hoard, no tendency to cause any change at all in the price of non-liquid assets. (Keynes, 1973a, p. 224)

The "repercussions on the aggregate propensity to hoard" that he actually considers in the *Treatise* (pp. 147–9) are precisely those which would arise from a dependence of $L$ on $Q$.

That Keynes thought he was propounding a general theory of the temporary-equilibrium level of interest rates, not a special case, is apparent from later passages in "A rejoinder":

Let us, for the moment, assume with Mr Robertson that the savers dispose of their savings, into liquid or non-liquid assets as the case may be, before the losing entrepreneurs have time to provide for their losses. (In a sense this is an impossible assumption, since in a sense the two things must take place simultaneously. The first stage must necessarily be that the savers find themselves with more money, and the losers find themselves with less money. But we will allow the savers to "get in first" in the sense of allowing them to decide whether or not to embark this money in non-liquid assets, before the losers have time to decide whether or not to make up their cash deficiency by selling non-liquid assets.) (Keynes, 1973a, pp. 227–8)

Then, if the savers purchase non-liquid assets, the prices of such assets will have to rise.

But this increase will only last so long as the telephone girls, attached to the exchange to which the losing entrepreneurs belong, persist in giving them wrong numbers. As soon as they can get through, they will sell non-liquid assets to the same amount as the excess savers have been previously buying them – that is, unless the hoarding propensities of the savers are different from the hoarding propensities of the entrepreneurs, and the effect of these sales will be to bring non-liquid assets back again to their previous price . . . Indeed, it seems to me that it would be absurd to suppose that the final result can depend on the order in which two transactions take place, which are, in the nature of the case, nearly simultaneous and each of which is as likely as the other to come first. The essential point, which I maintain and Mr Robertson resists, is the fact that an increase of saving which is not associated with an increase of investment does not change in any way either the quantity of assets or the quantity of purchasing power, but merely transfers command over cash in the first instance, and the ownership of assets after there has been time to reduce individual cash holdings to a normal level, between one set of persons and another set, i.e. between the saving public and the disappointed entrepreneurs. (Keynes, 1973a, pp. 229–30)

Evidence that the same doctrine survived in the *General Theory* and after (and incidentally that the temporary equilibrium relative to a given output also survived) is provided in his letter to Hawtrey, 6 March 1936 (Keynes, 1973b, p. 12): "Apart from indirect effects of repercussions, the rate of investment has no influence to affect the price of securities, since the demand for securities rises and falls by precisely the same amount as supply, unless other factors are changing."

The title of the controversy is obviously inappropriate. It was attached by economists who, conceiving the *IS–LM* equilibrium, or its full-employment counterpart, as the economy's temporary equilibrium, thought that Keynes must have been denying that the rate of interest's passage to its equilibrium value was determined by the higgling in the market for loanable funds. For in that equilibrium, if the markets for goods and loanable funds are cleared, the average demand for money is equal to the supply. Indeed Hicks (1939, p. 153), looking at the controversy from that standpoint, called it a sham dispute about which of $n+1$ equations to eliminate, via Walras' law, in determining $n$ prices. But the controversy arose in the context of a temporary equilibrium with a given output, not in the context of the *IS-LM* equilibrium. Keynes had not even invented the *IS-LM* equilibrium when he first formulated his theory of interest.

In point of fact the answer to the question whether $\alpha$ is positive or zero, like the answer to the question how deposits are created, is crucial for the theory of aggregate demand, as we shall now demonstrate.

## Mathematical Appendix

We shall prove that, if $X_g$ and $X_f$ are continuously differentiable functions of $Q$ and $r$, and if the inequalities (1.20), (1.21), and (1.22) are everywhere satisfied, an equilibrium is unique, and is asymptotically stable regardless of the relative magnitudes of $\epsilon_g$ and $\epsilon_f$.

*Proof of Uniqueness*  Let us abbreviate by suppressing the parameters, writing for (1.12) and (1.17) respectively

$$X_g = G(Q, r)$$

$$X_f = G(Q, r) + \alpha Q + \beta[kL(Q, r) - R],$$

where $G(Q, r)$ is $I(Q, r) - S(Q, r) - Q$. An equilibrium is a zero of this mapping from $\mathbb{R}^2$ into $\mathbb{R}^2$. The mapping is continuously differentiable in an open rectangular region. Its Jacobian matrix is

$$\mathbf{J} = \begin{bmatrix} G_Q & G_r \\ (G_Q + \alpha + \beta k L_Q) & (G_r + \beta k L_r) \end{bmatrix}.$$

The inequalities (1.20), (1.21), and (1.22) are:

$$G_Q < 0, \quad G_r + \beta k L_r < 0,$$

$$\det \mathbf{J} = \beta k G_Q L_r - (\alpha + \beta k L_Q) G_r) > 0.$$

Since $\mathbf{J}$ is an $N$–$P$-matrix (the principal minors of odd order are negative and that of even order is positive), the mapping is one-to-one. (See Nikaidô, 1968, p. 361, Definition 20.3, and p. 371, Corollary to theorem 20.4). ∎

*Proof of Asymptotic Stability* The adjustment to equilibrium is governed by the system of differential equations:

$$\dot{Q} = \epsilon_g G(Q, r)$$

$$\dot{r} = \epsilon_f [G(Q, r) + \alpha Q + \beta k L(Q, r) - R],$$

which are continuously differentiable in $Q$ and $r$. The matrix of coefficients of the linear approximation around the equilibrium $(Q^*, r^*)$ is

$$\mathbf{A} = \begin{bmatrix} \epsilon_g G_Q & \epsilon_g G_r \\ \epsilon_f (G_Q + \alpha + \beta k L_Q) & \epsilon_f (G_r + \beta k L_r) \end{bmatrix}$$

with

$$\mathrm{tr}\ \mathbf{A} = \epsilon_g G_Q + \epsilon_f (G_r + \beta k L_r)$$

$$\det \mathbf{A} = \epsilon_g \epsilon_f [\beta k G_Q L_r - (\alpha + \beta k L_Q) G_r].$$

Therefore the same inequalities imply $\mathrm{tr}\ \mathbf{A} < 0$ and $\det \mathbf{A} > 0$ for all positive $\epsilon_g$ and $\epsilon_f$. ∎

Finally, we prove that, if $\alpha$ is positive, $r^*$ is greater or less than it would be with $\alpha$ zero, according to whether $I^* - S^* = Q^*$ is positive or negative.

*Proof* Differentiating the temporary-equilibrium equations

$$G(Q^*, r^*) = 0$$
$$\alpha Q^* + \beta [kL(Q^*, r^*) - R] = 0$$

with respect to $\alpha$ and applying Cramer's Rule, we find

$$\frac{dr^*}{d\alpha} = -\frac{Q^* G_Q}{\det \mathbf{J}}.$$

Since $G_Q$ is negative and $\det \mathbf{J}$ is positive, sign $dr^*/d\alpha = -$ sign $Q^*$, i.e. $r^*$ increases or decreases with $\alpha$ according to whether $Q^*$ is positive or negative. Therefore it is higher than its value at $\alpha = 0$ if $Q^*$ is positive, and lower than that value if $Q^*$ is negative. ∎

## Notes

1    Under the alternative assumption of derivative deposits the commercial banks will have their desired ratio of reserves to deposits, and the need for active net

hoarding will be imposed on the public, not on the banks. Its extent may be assumed to be $\gamma(L-D)$, where $\gamma > 0$ is an adjustment coefficient and $D=R/k$. The flow excess-demand function for money deflated by $pK$ will then be

$$X_m = \alpha Q + \gamma[L(Q, r; x, \lambda) - R/k], \tag{1.15}'$$

and the flow excess-demand function for loanable funds follows from this equation together with (1.12) and (1.16).

2   It is not strictly necessary that $r$ should be positive. For, first, it need not be the rate at which perpetual real "cash flows" are discounted and, secondly, if the demand for deposits depends on the difference between $r$ and average real deposit rates, it need not become perfectly elastic at $r=0$, since average real deposit rates may be negative.

3   In the *Treatise* Keynes uses $E$ for "*the community's* [expected] *money-income*" excluding windfall profits (pp. 123–4 and p. 135); $O$ for "total output" (p. 135), which is our $Y$; and $\Pi$ for "the price level of output as a whole" (p. 137), which is our $\Pi$. His equation for the price level of output as a whole is

$$\Pi = E/O + (I-S)/O.$$

$I$ is "the value of new investment" (p. 138), which is the same as our $KpI^*$, since actual and planned investment are equal when markets are cleared. $S$ is "the sum of the differences between the money-incomes of individuals [$E$] and their money-expenditure on current consumption." If, as he later assumed, the employment of labor depends on short-term expectations, his $E$ becomes our $pY$ and his $S$ becomes our $KpS^*$. Substitution of these terms of ours in his equation then yields our (1.25).

4   Under the assumption of derivative deposits (1.24) is replaced by the equation

$$\alpha Q^* = \gamma[R/k - L(Q, r^*; x, \lambda)]. \tag{1.24}'$$

Passive net hoarding of windfalls is balanced by active net dishoarding by the public.

5   In the case of derivative deposits equation (1.26) becomes

$$\alpha[I(Q^*, r^*; x) - S(Q^*, r^*; x)] = \gamma[R/k - L(Q^*, r^*; x, \lambda)]. \tag{1.26}'$$

The portion of $I^* - S^*$ that is not matched financially by net loans from windfalls must be matched by funds arising from the public's active net dishoarding of deposits. Given the average demand for deposits and the stock of them created by the banking system, such active net dishoarding "today" is sustained by the passive net hoarding of "yesterday." Thus in this case too the flow of funds accommodating "today's" $\alpha(I^* - S^*)$ is "yesterday's" passive net hoarding of windfalls.

6   Notice that this must be so, no matter which view one takes on the genesis of deposits.

# 2

# The Theory of Aggregate Demand

If "Say's law of markets" is the assertion that markets operate so as always to prohibit general "gluts" and "dearths," meaning differences between aggregate money demand for final outputs and the sum of money incomes in the expectation of which the outputs have been produced (the expected costs of production), the controversy over it has long been resolved with the general-glut theorists victorious. Nevertheless there remains a question still unresolved, which may well be regarded as the fundamental question in the theory of aggregate demand, namely whether, by following the simple *non-discretionary* policy of accommodating the member banks, on terms determined by the market, with whatever reserves they demand, the central bank can ensure that the free play of market forces will indeed equate aggregate money demand to the sum of expected money incomes. If so, Say's law of markets can, after all, be invoked and rescinded whenever we wish.

As we shall see, this is not an entirely new idea. But it is not commonly regarded as a respectable one. Monetary economics has proceeded for many years under the supposition that the aggregate money demand for final output must be a determinant of the economy's behavior unless discretionary policies can succeed in neutralizing it. Most, but not all, of the theories that we shall be considering take this for granted.

Accordingly the object of this chapter is twofold: to specify the requirements for the success of such a policy, and to record the objections to it which have been stated or implied by some leading members of the opposition.

## 2.1 The Conditions for Say's Law

### I The Market Clearing Conditions

It must be assumed, as we have hitherto assumed, that the markets for goods and for loanable funds are always cleared; otherwise there is insufficient scope for the play of market forces.

## II The Existence of a Zero-Q Equilibrium

It must be supposed that, for each pair of values of the parameters $x$ and $\lambda$, there is a stock or reserves with which the equations of temporary equilibrium would be

$$I(0, r^*; x) = S(0, r^*; x) \tag{2.1}$$

$$kL(0, r^*; x, \lambda) = R^* \tag{2.2}$$

$$\pi^* = p. \tag{2.3}$$

The feature of this particular temporary equilibrium is that the net sum of windfall profits is zero or, equivalently, that the average of market prices equals the average expectation of them entertained at the outset of the instant. Consequently aggregate money demand $pK(I^* + C^*) \equiv p[Y + K(I^* - S^*)]$ and money income $\pi^* Y$ are equal to, and indeed determined by, the parametrically given sum of expected money incomes $pY$. This determination has been accomplished by the establishment of a general level of interest rates that equates investment to planned saving. To put the matter in Wicksellian terms, market rates of interest are also "normal" rates, "at which *the demand for loan capital and the supply of savings* exactly agree" (Wicksell, 1934, p. 193).

If such an $R^*$, which, of course, depends on the parameters, could not only be found but also sustained from instant to instant, however the parameters might be changing, movements of aggregate money demand would have no effect on the economy, since they would themselves be the effect of changes in the sum of expected money incomes. Inflation, fluctuations, unemployment there might be, but none of them due to movements of the aggregate money demand for output.

## III Commercial Banks Subject to the Law of Reflux

We have already stated the case for this theory of the genesis of deposits. But we also observed that its successful operation depends on the clearing of all submarkets for funds. If, for example, the market for bank loans failed to clear because of ceilings imposed on loan rates, credit rationing could deprive the public of deposits it wished to have. Therefore it must be assumed that no such limitations are in force.

## IV  The Central Bank Imposes a Law of Reflux on Itself

In these circumstances the central bank is able to subject itself to a law of reflux for reserves. Instead of controlling member banks' cash reserves by active trading in securities at their current prices, it can stand passively ready to deal in them with the banks, still at their current prices, in exchange for reserves, or to alter the volume of its loans to them, at current interest rates, acting as lender of *first* resort, not merely *last* resort.

*This is the non-discretionary rule to be followed by a central bank wishing to impose Say's law.* So long as the rule is in force, the member banks can alter their reserves to any desired extent by trading securities with it.

Since under the law of reflux in commercial banking the member banks cannot create derivative deposits, their only motive for changing their reserves is to bring them into equality with $kD=kL$. Both convenience and economic incentive will induce the member banks to accomplish their net hoarding via the central bank, the incentive being the tendency of security prices to move against them if they go to the market instead. By the end of each instant not only the public but also the commercial banks will have the amount of money they wish to hold on the average.

## V  Passive Net Hoarding of Windfalls

Given the conditions *I* to *IV*, the system of equations leading to a temporary equilibrium with parametric reserves is replaced by a system consisting of the three excess-demand functions.

$$X_g = I(Q, r; x) - S(Q, r; x) - Q \tag{1.12}$$

$$X_m = \alpha Q \tag{2.4}$$

$$X_f = X_g + X_m, \tag{1.16}$$

the two laws of reflux,

$$L(Q, r; x, \lambda) = D \tag{2.5}$$

$$R = kD,$$ (2.6)

and the market adjustments,

$$\dot{Q} = \epsilon_g X_g$$ (1.13)

$$\dot{r} = \epsilon_f X_f.$$ (1.18)

An equilibrium $(Q^*, r^*, D^*, R^*)$ is a rest point of this system, or equivalently a zero of any two of the three excess-demand functions, together with (2.5) and (2.6). Putting $X_g = X_m = 0$ we obtain

$$Q^* = I(Q^*, r^*; x) - S(Q^*, r^*; x)$$ (1.23)

$$\alpha Q^* = 0$$ (2.7)

$$L(Q^*, r^*; x, \lambda) = D^*$$ (2.8)

$$R^* = kD^*.$$ (2.9)

But, under the assumption that there is passive net hoarding of windfalls, that is, that $\alpha$ is positive, the only solution to these equations is the zero-$Q$ equilibrium of $(2.1) - (2.3)$.

*VI  Higher Interest Rates Imply a Lower $I - S$*

It is easily shown that this equilibrium entails a unique $r^*$, and that it is asymptotically stable, whatever the speeds of adjustment $\epsilon_g$ and $\epsilon_f$ may be, if the inequalities

$$I_Q - S_Q - 1 < 0$$ (1.20)

$$\alpha(I_r - S_r) < 0$$ (2.10)

are satisfied, where (2.10) is implied by Conditions V and VI. The proof is in the Appendix to this chapter.

The logic of the situation is simple enough. If there is some passive net hoarding of windfalls, the market can support a non-zero $I^* - S^*$ only if the banks fill the financial gap by active net dishoarding. But since, under the assumed policy of the central bank, the commercial banks obtain from it just the reserves they need, there is no net supply of loanable funds from this source, therefore, rates of interest must be such as to close the gap by making $I^* = S^*$. The market mechanism itself will ensure that aggregate supply $pY$ creates its own demand by bringing about a complex of interest rates at which planned saving and investment are equal.

Actually if Condition IV were replaced by the assumption that there is no central bank and that all money consists of the notes and deposits of *non-colluding* commercial banks holding each others' deposits as reserves, then (given the other requirements) formally speaking Say's law would always rule. For in the above equations, if $R=k=0$, then $Q^*=0$. There is room, however, for skepticism concerning the viability of such a monetary system. There is also room for questioning the desirability of invoking Say's law in such a way as to forego the option of rescinding it.

## 2.2 Antagonists

A complete history of the opposition to this idea would fill volumes. Moreover the opponents have not spoken with one voice. I have chosen, therefore, to quote from certain leading authorities representing distinct lines of resistance to it.

### Thornton

One of the arguments in Thornton's *Paper Credit* was directed against "those who have been in the habit of deeming all limitation of the bank paper by the bank itself to be unnecessary" (Thornton, 1939, p. 230). The context shows that "the bank" referred to is the Bank of England. The question at issue was precisely that of the efficacy of the policy which we have been considering, namely (p. 251) "whether those bounds within which Bank of England paper must be confined, in order to guard against a dangerous depreciation of it, are likely to be observed, in consequence of some natural tendency which it has to limit itself, so that it is unnecessary that the bank should restrain it." Thornton's argument against such a natural tendency is to be found on pp. 253-5:

It only remains to enquire, lastly, whether any principle of moderation and forbearance on the part of the borrowers at the bank may be likely to exempt the directors of that institution from the necessity of imposing their own limit. It may possibly be thought, that a liberal extension of loans would soon satisfy all demands, and that the true point at which the encrease of the paper ought to stop, would be discovered by the unwillingness of the merchants to continue borrowing. In order to ascertain how far the desire of obtaining loans at the bank may be expected at any time to be carried, we must enquire into the subject of the quantum of profit likely to be derived from borrowing there under the existing circumstances. This is to be judged of by considering two points: the amount, first of interest to be paid on the sum borrowed; and, secondly, of the mercantile or other gain to be obtained by the employment of the borrowed capital. The gain which can be acquired by the means of commerce is commonly the highest which can be had; and it also regulates, in a great measure, the rate in all other cases. We may, therefore, consider this question as turning principally on a comparison of the rate of interest taken at the bank with the current rate of mercantile profit. The bank is prohibited, by the state of the law, from demanding, even in time of war, an interest of more than five per cent., which is the same rate at which it discounts in a period of profound peace. (Thornton, 1939 pp. 253–4)

Thornton's objection was that the legally imposed ceiling on the central bank's discount rate would thwart the policy's objective whenever it became binding (p. 255). For in the first place it would create an excess demand for loans. Condition I above would be violated: "The borrowers, in consequence of that artificial state of things which is produced by the law against usury, obtain their loans too cheap. That which they obtain too cheap they demand in too great a quantity." In the second place artificially low interest rates would afford borrowers artificially high profits. These profits would have the effect of drawing more money into circulation and raising prices. But at the higher prices "the temptation to borrow at five per cent. will be exactly the same as before;" so that the process of monetary expansion would continue.

The argument can be sketched formally as follows. Suppose that the legal ceiling on interest rates, $r_c$, say, is below the level that would rule in the zero-$Q$ temporary equilibrium, namely the $r^*$ that satisfies equation (2.1). This need not preclude the clearing of the market for final output when the constraint is binding, but, given that the central bank is imposing on itself the law of reflux, it must then preclude the clearing of the market for loanable funds. Thus if the constraint is binding, we shall have, from $X_g = 0$ with $r = r_c$,

$$Q^* = I(Q^*, r_c; x) - S(Q^*, r_c; x). \tag{2.11}$$

and from (2.4), which is the flow excess demand for money when the two laws of reflux are in force,

$$X_m = \alpha Q^* = \alpha(I^* - S^*). \tag{2.12}$$

Since $I_r - S_r$ is negative, (2.11) implies a larger $Q^*$ than that which solves (2.1), that is, a positive $Q^*$, so that (2.12) together with Walras' law implies an excess demand for loanable funds. There is a fringe of unsatisfied borrowers at the artificially low level of interest rates. Thus when the ceiling on interest rates is binding, the result of the central bank's policy is a positive sum of windfall profits (an aggregate money demand exceeding the sum of expected money incomes), and a permanent excess demand for funds. Moreover the persistence of this situation from one instant to another will be expansionary, inducing upward revisions of expected incomes, so that more and more reserves and deposits will be drawn into circulation to support ever-increasing money incomes per unit of capital, viz. $p[f(x) + Q^*]$.

Nevertheless Thornton was of the opinion that, if the law imposing this ceiling were repealed, the policy would be not only effective but also, he implied, desirable (p. 254): "It might, undoubtedly, at all seasons, sufficiently limit its paper by means of the price at which it lends, if the legislature did not interpose an obstacle to the constant adoption of this principle of restriction."

## Keynes

In the *General Theory* (1936, pp. 18–22) Keynes accused not only the "classical" economists but also some of his contemporaries (mentioning especially Lionel Robbins) of "fallaciously supposing that there is a nexus which unites decisions to abstain from present consumption with decisions to provide for future consumption . . . [so that] the aggregate demand price is equal to the aggregate supply price for all levels of output and employment." His chapter 14 entitled "The classical theory of the rate of interest" is devoted to demolishing the idea that in a monetary economy "the rate of interest necessarily comes to rest under the play of market forces at the point where the amount of investment at that rate of interest is equal to the amount of saving at that rate" (p. 175), and, by implication, also the weaker claim that it could be induced to do so "without the necessity for any special intervention or grand-motherly care on the part of the monetary authority" (p. 177).

The gist of the argument was that in the absence of special intervention the system would not contain enough equations to determine both interest rates and the level of income (pp. 179–83). Indeed, this position does follow inexorably, within the context of the non-discretionary policy we have stipulated, from Keynes's refusal (or inability) to contemplate the possibility of passive net hoarding (Condition V), from which his liquidity-preference theory of interest was derived. If $\alpha$ is zero, the equation

$$\alpha Q^* = 0 \tag{2.7}$$

does not imply $Q^* = 0$. Instead, the equilibrium equations of our dynamic system with the two laws of reflux have a multiplicity of solutions. The zero-$Q$ equilibrium is among them; but it is easily established (see the Appendix) that in its neighborhood there is a continuous locus of others, in all of which $Q^*$ is non-zero. Therefore the zero-$Q$ equilibrium cannot be asymptotically stable. The central bank's rule would not impose Say's law. It would merely render indeterminate the complex of interest rates and the sum of money incomes at which $I^* - S^*$ would be matched financially by net loans from windfalls. We may conclude, therefore, that Keynes was logically committed to rejecting the efficacy of our policy rule, even though he never explicitly considered it.

## Extreme Keynesians

Those who originally interpreted Keynes's case against Say's law did not, in fact, reproduce it. Instead, they formulated the "extreme Keynesian" argument that at least over some range of values of $x$ no equilibrium complex of interest rates is consistent with the equality of planned saving and investment. The possibility of validating the "classical" theory of interest by monetary policy is ruled out either by a failure of $I$ and $S$ to respond to changes in $r$ or by a "liquidity trap". In either case there is a failure of our Condition II. In particular this occurs at that value of $x$ which corresponds to full employment in a short-period equilibrium.

The liquidity-trap argument appears in Hicks:

This brings us to what, from many points of view, is the most important thing in Mr Keynes' book. It is not only possible to show that a given supply of money determines a certain relation between Income and interest (which we have expressed by the curve *LL*); it is also possible to say something about the shape of the curve. It will probably tend to be nearly horizontal on the left . . . [because there is] some minimum below which the rate of interest is unlikely to go . . . If the costs of holding money can be neglected, it will always be profitable to hold money rather than lend it out, if the rate of interest is greater than zero. Consequently the rate of interest must always be positive . . . If *IS* lies to the right, then we can indeed increase employment by increasing the quantity of money; but if *IS* lies to the left, we cannot do so; merely monetary means will not force down the rate of interest any further. (Hicks, 1937, pp. 154–5)

But the argument is not compelling. Why should there not be a cost of holding money? Rates of interest on deposits can be negative, and the risk of theft discourages large holdings of currency.

The other argument is more interesting, since it is quite possible, as we have noted previously, that $I-S$ will not be much affected by $r$. Also it does not depend on the economy's being in a depressed state. One of the earliest statements of it is in Klein:

The simplest Keynesian theory is the following: Savings as a function of the level of income equals autonomous investment. This is one equation in one variable, namely the level of income. Investment is considered to be autonomous because it depends upon such factors as the expectations of future market demand, innovations, fiscal policy, etc. It is obvious, however, that the validity of the Keynesian theory does not depend on the fact that investment is autonomous, for, if investment is also a function of income, the Keynesian theory of the savings-investment determination of income still holds. (Klein, 1947, p. 110)

At about the same time, however, the same argument was put forward by Tobin (1947, p. 576) as a reason why reducing money wages might fail to stimulate aggregate demand.

## Tobin

In more recent times Keynes's own case against the possibility of establishing Say's law by monetary policy seems to have been implicit in Tobin's general equilibrium model of asset yields (Tobin, 1969). For he there assumed both that commercial bank deposits are always equal to the demand for them (p. 27) and that rates of interest are determined by the conditions of stock equilibrium in financial markets without regard to the conditions of flow equilibrium in the market for final output (p. 16). The asset stock equilibrium by which rates of interest are determined "corresponds to any tentative assumption about aggregate real income and the commodity price level" (p. 16).

But in his Nobel lecture (Tobin, 1982) he appears to have withdrawn from this position. Asset prices and real income (or the price level) are simultaneously determined by flow conditions in a short-period equilibrium. Something still prevents him from contemplating the possibility of Say's law, but since we are not told what situation would prevail in asset markets if planned investment and planned saving were not equal, it is impossible to say what that something is.

### Monetarists

Ignoring the numerous other connotations of this term, I use it merely as a label for those who reject the law of reflux in commercial banking (Condition III) and believe that the banks create derivative deposits.

As we observed in the last chapter, while Keynes himself gave an exposition of the derivative deposit doctrine in chapter 2 of the *Treatise*, his account, in chapter 17 of the same work, of the mechanism whereby changes in central bank reserves alter the total of deposits was quite consistent with the law of reflux. Moreover his argument against the possibility of establishing the "classical" theory of interest was entirely based on his liquidity-preference theory. Perhaps we should conclude that for him the automatic equation of planned saving to investment is out of reach no matter how the quantity of deposits is determined.

But it seems fair to say that the chief objection in the twentieth century to the idea that Say's law is available if we want it has been acceptance of the doctrine of derivative deposits. Indeed, most of Keynes's contemporaries were just as much opposed to the idea as he was, despite their having been on the "loanable-funds" side of the debate about the theory of interest.

For example, Robertson (1928, reprinted 1940), had this to say in a lecture on theories of banking policy:

My *second proposition* is the time-worn one that this bank-money comes into existence mainly as the result of loans and investments made by the banking system, and that consequently, in most circumstances, the proximate force determining its amount is a series of decisions made by some person or persons situated with the banking system . . . I should not have thought it worth while to assert this truism in the shape of a formal proposition, were it not that a widespread feeling among bankers that they are being "got at" in some way by orthodox teaching on this matter has induced even so eminent an authority as the late Walter Leaf to use language which is cloudy and misleading. If anybody retains any lingering doubts on this matter, whether these doubts arise from consideration of the multiplicity of banks or from some less rational cause, I commend to him the careful and patient article of Mr Crick on "The Genesis of Bank Deposits" in *Economica*, June 1927. (Robertson, 1940, p. 41)

While he goes on to qualify this by admitting that under certain conditions the banks may not be able to persuade the public to borrow, the qualification does not prevent him from conducting his formal analysis of the theory of interest (Robertson, 1940, pp. 1–38) under the derivative-deposit hypothesis. The "net dis-hoardings" which he lists among the terms comprising the net supply of loanable funds (p. 3) are past savings of money now being withdrawn from store, less current savings of money now being put into store. They are therefore carried out by the public, not by the banks.

One can infer without recourse to formal analysis that, if the member banks create derivative deposits, the policy of supplying them with whatever reserves they wanted would lead not to Say's law but to an indefinite expansion of money incomes. For, since there is a positive probability that the derivative deposits created by any bank will not all be lost to other banks, they all have an incentive to sell securities to the central bank for extra reserves and to buy securities in the market or extend loans in excess of the extra reserves. $R$ and $D$ would expand indefinitely so long as the banks could find profitable investments for extra deposits.

## 2.3 Conclusion

Among the various objections which we have considered the weakest seem to be both that of Keynes himself and that of the monetarists. The others are at least logically respectable. However, since I have committed myself to the assumption of temporary equilibrium, I must rule out of court objections based on a failure of market forces. My attitude is that one should be loth to dispense with market clearing except where there is some phenomenon (such as fluctuations of the unemployment percentage around its average level) which cannot easily be explained under this rubric.

**Mathematical Appendix**

Using the notation of the appendix to chapter 1, we shall prove that, if the inequalities given under Condition VI above are satisfied, an equilibrium of the dynamic system presented under Condition V is unique, and is asymptotically stable for all speeds of adjustment.

*Proof of Uniqueness*   The excess-demand functions are

$$X_g = G(Q, r)$$

$$X_m = \alpha Q$$

$$X_f = G(Q, r) + \alpha Q.$$

The two laws of reflux are combined in

$$kL(Q, r) = R.$$

We shall suppose that there is a solution $(0, r^*,)$, with $r^* > 0$, to the equations $X_g = X_m = 0$. It is a zero of the mapping from $\mathbb{R}^2$ into $\mathbb{R}^2$

$$-G(Q, r)$$

$$-\alpha Q.$$

Let the mapping be continuously differentiable in an open rectangular region. Its Jacobian matrix is

$$\mathbf{J} = \begin{bmatrix} -G_Q & -G_r \\ -\alpha & 0 \end{bmatrix}.$$

If the following inequalities hold throughout the region:

$$G_Q < 0,$$

$$\det \mathbf{J} = -\alpha G_r > 0,$$

the mapping is one-to-one and the solution is unique, since $\mathbf{J}$ is a weak $P$-matrix (see Nikaidô, 1968, pp. 376–7). Then there is also a unique

$$R^* = L(0, r^*),$$

so that the triplet $(0, r^*, R^*)$ is the only equilibrium obeying the two laws of reflux.

*Proof of Asymptotic Stability*   The differential equations are

$$\dot{Q} = \epsilon_g G(Q, r)$$

$$\dot{r} = \epsilon_f [G(Q, r) + \alpha Q]$$

The matrix of coefficients of the linear approximation around the equilibrium $(Q^*, r^*)$ is

$$\mathbf{B} = \begin{bmatrix} \epsilon_g G_Q & \epsilon_g G_r \\ \epsilon_f (G_Q + \alpha) & \epsilon_f G_r \end{bmatrix}$$

with

$$\text{tr } \mathbf{B} = \epsilon_g G_Q + \epsilon_f G_r$$

$$\det \mathbf{B} = -\epsilon_g \epsilon_f \alpha G_r.$$

Therefore the inequalities implying uniqueness also imply tr $\mathbf{B} < 0$ and det $\mathbf{B} > 0$ for all positive $\epsilon_g$ and $\epsilon_f$.

Finally we show that, if $\alpha$ is zero, the zero-$Q$ equilibrium cannot be asymptotically stable.

*Proof*   When $\alpha = 0$ the equilibrium equations become

$$G(Q^*, r^*) = 0$$

$$kL(Q^*, r^*) = R^*.$$

If $(0, r^*, R^*)$ is a solution, there is a continuous locus of others in its neighborhood, in all of which $Q^*$ is non-zero. For since $G_Q$ and $G_r$ are negative, we have $dQ^*/dr^* = -G_r/G_Q < 0$ at the zero-$Q^*$ equilibrium point. If, therefore, there is a displacement from $(0, r^*, R^*)$, there is no reason why there should be a return to it.

# 3

# A General Framework for Aggregative Dynamics

Since this is not a book on mathematical methods, it would be intolerably tedious to be precise about the continuity and differentiability of the functions we shall use. Suffice it to say that henceforth they will be assumed to possess whatever analytical properties the arguments may call for.

### 3.1 The Dependence of the Temporary Equilibrium on its Parameters

The movement of the temporary equilibrium from one instant to the next is governed by dynamic forces acting on its parameters. As a preliminary to understanding the working out of these forces we must express the equilibrium as a function of its parameters and discover what can be said about its response to changes in them, its comparative statics.

The principal dependent variables we shall want to know about are windfall profits ($Q^*$) and capital accumulation ($\dot{K}/K$).

### Temporary Equilibrium with Parametric Reserves

When the central bank determines reserves at the outset of each instant, the variables depend on the vector of parameters $(x, \lambda, R/k)$; for $R$ is parametric and $k$ is a constant. $R/k$ is the 'potential' supply of deposits deflated by $pK$. We shall refer to it as (*the supply of*) *real balances*. For convenience let us write

$$R/k = m = zf'(x), \tag{3.1}$$

where $z$ is the potential supply of deposits deflated by $wK$ instead of $pK$, (*the supply of*) *real balances in terms of wage units*. It will sometimes be convenient to work in terms of $z$ instead of $m$. Also additional parameters will subsequently become relevant. But in this chapter let us confine our attention to the influence of $x$, $\lambda$, and $m$.

*Windfall Profits*    The equations determining the temporary-equilibrium values of $Q^*$ and $r^*$ are

$$Q^* = I(Q^*, r^*; x) - S(Q^*, r^*; x) \tag{1.23}$$

$$\alpha Q^* = \gamma[m - L(Q^*, r^*; x, \lambda)]. \tag{3.2}$$

Equation (3.2) is obtained from (1.24) by defining

$$\gamma = \beta k \tag{3.3}$$

If, however, one accepts the doctrine of derivative deposits, (3.2) is obtained directly by putting $R/k = m$ in (1.24)' (ch. 1, note 4).

We shall suppose that the equations imply functions

$$Q^* = Q^*(x, m, \lambda) \tag{3.4}$$

$$r^* = r^*(x, m, \lambda) \tag{3.5}$$

for all meaningful values of their arguments. Differentiating (1.23) and (3.2) we obtain

$$\Delta Q_x^* = \gamma[(I_r - S_r)L_x - L_r(I_x - S_x)], \tag{3.6}$$

$$\Delta Q_m^* = -\gamma(I_r - S_r), \tag{3.7}$$

$$\Delta Q_\lambda^* = \gamma(I_r - S_r)L_\lambda, \tag{3.8}$$

$$\Delta r_x^* = (\alpha + \gamma L_Q)(I_x - S_x) - \gamma(I_Q - S_Q - 1)L_x, \tag{3.9}$$

$$\Delta r_m^* = \gamma(I_Q - S_Q - 1), \tag{3.10}$$

$$\Delta r_\lambda^* = -\gamma(I_Q - S_Q - 1)L_\lambda, \tag{3.11}$$

where, by (1.20), (1.21), (1.22), and (3.3), the inequalities

$$I_Q - S_Q - 1 < 0 \tag{1.20}$$

$$I_r - S_r + \gamma L_r < 0 \tag{1.21}'$$

$$\Delta = \gamma(I_Q - S_Q - 1)L_r - (\alpha + \gamma L_Q)(I_r - S_r) > 0 \tag{1.22}'$$

are satisfied for all values of the parameters. (Each market is stable on its own, and each market is stable when the other market is cleared.)

But stability conditions alone are not enough to exclude bizarre possibilities. To that end we need four more inequalities:

$$L_r \leq 0 \text{ and } L_\lambda \leq 0, \tag{3.12}$$

$$I_r - S_r \leq 0, \tag{3.13}$$

$$\alpha + \gamma L_Q \geq 0. \tag{3.14}$$

Other things being equal, a rise in real interest rates or in expected inflation does not increase the demand for deposits; a rise in real interest rates does not increase the excess demand for goods; and a rise in net windfalls does not diminish the flow excess demand for money.

With the aid of these seven inequalities definite statements can be made about the signs of the partials with respect to $m$ and $\lambda$. An increase in $m$ reduces real rates of interest ($r_m^* < 0$). If the reduction increases the excess of planned investment over planned saving ($I_r - S_r < 0$), the net sum of windfall profits will rise ($Q_m^* > 0$). But if the reduction has no such effect ($I_r - S_r = 0$), the change in $m$ leaves windfalls unchanged ($Q_m^* = 0$). An increase in expected inflation will reduce real rates of interest ($r_\lambda^* < 0$) if it reduces the demand for money ($L_\lambda < 0$), but not otherwise. If it does, windfalls will rise (or fail to rise) just as they would after an increase in $m$.

The effect of an increase in $x$ on windfall profits is ambiguous. Indeed, it is quite possible that $Q_x^*$ will be positive, at least in some part of its domain. For the marginal inducement to invest may exceed the marginal propensity to save ($I_x - S_x$ may be positive), and/or an increase in $x$ may, by increasing confidence, reduce entrepreneurs' demand for liquidity ($L_x$ may be negative). Since, from (1.23),

$$Q_x^* = \frac{I_x - S_x + (I_r - S_r)r_x^*}{-(I_Q - S_Q - 1)}, \tag{3.15}$$

the condition $(I_r - S_r)L_x - L_r(I_x - S_x) > 0$ in equation (3.6) is equivalent to a positive numerator in (3.15). It therefore means that, when $x$ increases, for example, either a positive effect on $Q^*$ due to $I_x$ being greater than $S_x$ is not dominated by a negative effect on it due to higher interest rates; or a positive effect due to lower interest rates is not dominated by a negative effect due to $S_x$ being greater than $I_x$.

*The Accumulation of Capital*   When temporary-equilibrium prices are unexpectedly high, either there is unintentionally low real consumption ("forced saving"), or there is unintentionally low real investment. Quite probably there are both of these. Since the conditions for temporary equilibrium say nothing on this subject, it is necessary to make an assumption specifying just what the relation of $\dot{K}$ to $KI^*$ and $KS^*$ is to be.

I propose to assume – without too much loss of generality, I hope – that real consumption is equal to $K(C^*-Q^*)$ and real investment $\dot{K}$ is equal to $KI^*=K(S^*+Q^*)$. Unexpected prices cause "forced saving", but do not separate actual real investment $\dot{K}$ from planned real investment $KI^*$. For going to this extreme is a simple way of ensuring that (as one might expect in general) actual real investment depends on windfalls (via $S^*+Q^*$) even if planned real investment does not depend on them (even if $I_Q$ is zero). Therefore in the present case of parametric reserves we have

$$\dot{K}/K=I^*(x, m, \lambda), \tag{3.16}$$

with

$$I^*(x, m, \lambda)=I^*[Q(x, m, \lambda), r^*(x, m, \lambda); x], \tag{3.17}$$

by (1.10), (3.4), and (3.5). The partial derivatives are

$$I_x^*=I_x+I_QQ_x^*+I_rr_x^*, \tag{3.18}$$

$$I_m^*=I_QQ_m^*+I_rr_m^*, \tag{3.19}$$

$$I_\lambda^*=I_QQ_\lambda^*+I_rr_\lambda^*. \tag{3.20}$$

Equations (3.19) and (3.20) indicate that, if $|I_Q|$ is sufficiently small, the "normal" signs of $I_m^*$ and $I_\lambda^*$ will be positive. An increase in $m$ reduces $r$ (and "normally" so does an increase in $\lambda$), and so increases capital accumulation if $I_r$ is negative.

The response of accumulation to an increase in $x$ is uncertain. The sources of doubt are revealed when (3.9) is substituted into (3.18), to obtain

$$I_x^*=\frac{(\alpha+\gamma L_Q)(S_rI_x-I_rS_x)-\gamma(I_Q-S_Q-1)(I_rL_x-L_rI_x)}{\gamma(I_Q-S_Q-1)L_r-(\alpha+\gamma L_Q)(I_r-S_r)}+I_QQ_x^*. \tag{3.21}$$

Since any direct effect of $Q$ on planned investment is on planned investment in inventories, perhaps it is not unreasonable to suppose that $|I_Q|$ is small enough for the last term not to be of consequence for the direction in which $x$ moves *aggregate* accumulation.

Even so there is still ambiguity. Of the two terms in the quotient the first may be said to represent the "real" determinants of $I_x^*-I_Q Q_x^*$, that is, those which have nothing to do with the effect of $x$ on the demand for deposits. Except in the case where investment depends neither on $x$ nor on $r$ ($I_x=I_r=0$), the sign of $S_r I_x-I_r S_x$ will 'normally'' be positive. For it would fail to be so only if there were a backward-rising supply curve of saving ($S_r < 0$) and in addition a rise in $x$ caused a large increase in interest rates. If $\alpha+\gamma L_Q$ is positive, then, the first term is likely to be positive.

The second term in the quotient gives the determinants which do operate through the effect of $x$ on the demand for deposits. Except, again, in the case where $I_x=I_r=0$, their effect can be positive if $L_r$ is negative. A rise in $x$ will tend to increase investment if its direct effect due to a positive marginal inducement to invest ($I_x > 0$), is not overborne by higher interest rates from an increase in the demand for deposits ($L_x > 0$), and *a fortiori* if it reduces the demand for deposits ($L_x < 0$). But the possibility remains that the monetary influence of a rise in $x$ will be to reduce investment.

### The Tobin-Solow Special Case

In the case of the Tobin-Solow temporary equilibrium with parametric reserves

$$I^*=Q^*+S(Q^*,r^*;x) \tag{1.24}$$

$$\alpha Q^* = \gamma[m-L(Q^*,r^*;x,\lambda)] \tag{3.2}$$

$$r^*=f(x)-xf'(x) \tag{1.28}$$

we cannot allow both $\alpha$ and $L_Q$ to be zero; otherwise $Q^*$ would be indeterminate; therefore, by (3.14).

$$\alpha+\gamma L_Q > 0. \tag{3.14'}$$

In addition, since investment plans respond only to $f(x) - xf'(x) - r$, $I_Q$ is zero, and so by (1.20).

$$1+S_Q > 0. \tag{1.20'}$$

*Windfall Profits*   The partials of $Q^*(x, m, \lambda)$ are now

$$Q_x^* = [L_r x f''(x) - L_x] \gamma / (\alpha + \gamma L_Q) \qquad (3.6)'$$

$$Q_m^* = \gamma / (\alpha + \gamma L_Q) \qquad (3.7)'$$

$$Q_\lambda^* = -L_\lambda \gamma / (\alpha + \gamma L_Q). \qquad (3.8)'$$

$Q_m^*$ is now certainly positive, and $Q_\lambda^*$ is positive if $L_\lambda$ is negative. The downward pressure of an increase in $m$ (and likewise of an increase in $\lambda$) on interest rates encourages investment so much that windfalls are increased without any actual fall in interest rates. But the sign of $Q_x^*$ remains ambiguous. When $x$ is higher interest rates are higher. On that account windfalls tend to be higher if the demand for money is reduced (if $L_r$ is negative). But $L_x$ may be sufficiently positive to overcome this tendency.

*The Accumulation of Capital*   The partials of $I^*(x, m, \lambda)$ are

$$I_x^* = S_x - S_r x f''(x) + (1 + S_Q) Q_x^*. \qquad (3.21)'$$

$$I_m^* = (1 + S_Q) Q_m^* \qquad (3.19)'$$

$$I_\lambda^* = (1 + S_Q) Q_\lambda^* \qquad (3.20)'$$

$I_m^*$ is now certainly positive, and $I_\lambda^*$ is "normally" so. But the uncertainty surrounding the sign of $I_x^*$ remains.

*Temporary Equilibrium with Say's Law*

The equations for temporary equilibrium in this case, which was the subject of chapter 2, are simply

$$Q^* = 0 \qquad (3.22)$$

$$I(0, r^*; x) - S(0, r^*; x) = 0 \qquad (3.23)$$

$$m^* = L(0, r^*; x, \lambda). \qquad (3.24)$$

We assume that (3.23) implies that the function

$$r^* = r^*(x) \qquad (3.25)$$

exists for all positive $x$. Its derivative is

$$r_x^* = -\frac{(I_x - S_x)}{(I_r - S_r)}, \qquad (3.26)$$

which has the sign of $I_x - S_x$, since $I_r - S_r$ must be negative if Say's law is to rule. The significance of $r_x^*$ is that it helps to determine the effect of $x$ on the accumulation of capital,

$$\dot{K}/K = I^*(x) = I[0, r^*(x); x]. \tag{3.27}$$

In fact

$$I_x^* = I_r r_x^* + I_x = \frac{I_x S_r - I_r S_x}{(S_r - I_r)}, \tag{3.28}$$

which is the formula that would emerge if, in (3.21) above, one assumed that $L_r$, $L_x$ and $Q_x^*$ were all zero. Naturally enough, under Say's law only the "real" determinants of $I_x^*$ are present. We have already concluded that this expression is normally positive.[1]

### 3.2  Two Dynamic Assumptions

A particular theory is formed when equations are given which regulate the behavior of all the parameters. For the comparison of different theories it is necessary to specify only a proper subset of such equations, in order to obtain an open-ended construction which can serve as our basic framework. For this purpose we shall stipulate, in a rather general form, dynamic equations for the development of short-term normal prices and of efficiency wages.

### The Dynamics of Short-term Normal Prices

The index of expected, or short-term normal, prices $p$ is expected to change at the exponential rate $\lambda$ and will do so if the index of actual prices $\pi^*$ turns out to be equal to it, and if efficiency wages are changing at the rate $\lambda$. But if $\pi^*$ is not equal to $p$, or equivalently if $Q^*$ is not zero, there is a tendency for the average expectation to be revised in the direction of the difference. There may also be a reason to revise it if efficiency wages are changing by more, or less, than $\lambda$. For if firms are experiencing an unexpected change in their wage costs, they may expect prices in other industries to change in the same direction, diverting demand to or from their own industry. I shall call this factor *cost push*. The action of the three forces is expressed by the equation

$$\dot{p}/p=\lambda+H(Q^*)+\sigma(\dot{w}/w-\lambda).$$   (3.29)

$H(Q^*)$ is a sign-preserving and strictly increasing function, $\sigma$ is a constant, and

$$0 \leq \sigma \leq 1.$$   (3.30)

The provenance of the cost-push factor is Keynes's *Treatise on Money* (1930, Ch. 11, pp. 166–8) in a section concerned with the effect on the price level of "spontaneous" changes in efficiency earnings, that is, changes in $w$ which are not induced by the existence of windfall profits or losses (p. 168). Indeed, he took for granted the extreme case of *full cost push*, in which $\sigma$ is unity:

Let the reader observe that changes in the average rate of earnings have no direct tendency in themselves to bring about profits or losses, because – so long as the Currency Authority allows the change without attempting to counteract it – entrepreneurs will always be recouped for their changed outlay by the corresponding change in their receipts, which will result from the proportionate change in the price level. (Keynes, 1930, p. 167)

Since

$$\pi^*=p+pQ^*/f(x),$$   (1.29)

$\pi^*=p$ if and only if $Q^*=0$. Then equation (3.29) tells us that, when $Q^*$ is zero and nothing occurs to upset this state of affairs, then $\dot{\pi}^*/\pi^*=\dot{p}/p=\dot{w}/w$ if and only if $\sigma=1$.

To justify the idea that $\sigma=1$ we should need to assume that, when an entrepreneur experiences an unexpected rise or fall in his wage costs, he believes that *all* other prices will rise or fall proportionately. This seems unlikely, to say the least, but it is a logical possibility and should, therefore, be permitted in our general system.

## The Dynamics of Efficiency Wages

The index of efficiency wages $w$ is also expected to change at the exponential rate $\lambda$ and we shall assume that it will do so if (1) there is no net excess demand for labor, that is, if unemployment (plus redundancies) equals unfilled vacancies; and if also (2) short-term normal prices are changing at the rate $\lambda$. But if labor is in excess demand or supply, it may exert an upward or downward pressure on the index. Also changes in short-term normal prices by more or less than $\lambda$ may cause changes in $w$. I shall call this factor *wage indexation*, although it is intended to cover a wider set of possibilities than this term suggests. The action of the three forces is expressed by the equation

$$\dot{w}/w=\lambda+F(x/v)+\tau(\dot{p}/p-\lambda).\tag{3.31}$$

$F(x/v)$ is a non-decreasing function, and

$$F(1)=0.\tag{3.32}$$

Its argument,

$$x/v=N^d/N^s,\tag{3.33}$$

in agreement with the definitions of $x$ and $v$ given in chapter 1. $\tau$ is a constant, and

$$0 \leq \tau \leq 1.\tag{3.34}$$

There is, admittedly, no compelling reason why the value of $x/v$ at which $F=0$ should be where unemployment equals unfilled vacancies; for the pressures exerted by employers' organizations and labor unions need not counterbalance each other. But where the essential characteristics of the theories to be considered are not materially affected by neglecting such lopsidedness we shall simplify the formal models by assuming that $F(1)=0$.

The persistence of positive unemployment and vacancies when $x/v$ is unity is assumed to be mainly due to a continual flux, breaking up old jobs and creating new ones, together with an imperfect flow of information to workers and employers concerning the whereabouts of suitable vacancies on the one hand, and of suitable people to fill them on the other. But of course quits to search may also contribute to it.

The term "natural rate" was introduced by Friedman (1968) to designate the unemployment rate which pertains to the situation in which $F=0$. But this has turned out to be an elusive concept (see Haltiwanger, 1987), owing partly to the fact that the secular element in the unemployment rate is subject to change, and partly to the difficulty of separating secular and cyclical changes. For our purposes the important theoretical distinction is between equilibrium and disequilibrium rates, in the customary hope that it mimics the practical distinction between the (possibly moving) average rate and deviations from it.

We postulate that after a rise (or fall) in $x/v$ the unemployment rate adjusts rapidly to a new lower (or higher) level, allowing us to regard it, within obvious limits, as a decreasing function of $x/v$.

This complex of ideas was well expressed, if not originated, by Pigou. In his *Employment and Equilibrium* (1941), he says:

[W]hereas, if the system were not subject to disturbances, full employment would always exist, in actual fact, employment on the average falls short of full employment by a certain quantity attributable to the disturbances. For, of course, the system is subject to disturbances, friction is not absent and labour is not completely mobile. The percentage, which, on the average of good and bad times, employment constitutes of the available labour force, is not a hundred per cent, but some smaller percentage, approximating more closely to a hundred per cent the more nearly the ideal of a stable, frictionless and completely mobile system is approached. As I put it in my *Theory of Unemployment*: "With perfectly free competition among workpeople and labour perfectly mobile . . . there will always be at work a strong tendency for wage-rates to be so related to demand that everybody is employed. Hence, in stable conditions everyone will actually be employed. The implication is that such unemployment as exists at any time is due wholly to the fact that changes in demand conditions are continually taking place and that frictional resistances prevent the appropriate wage adjustments from being made instantaneously." This, it should be observed, does not imply that the percentage of unemployment among would-be wage-earners over the average of good and bad times is necessarily the same. It will only be the same so long as the economic setting as regards friction, mobility and so on is the same . . . When the percentage of [un]employment is heavy, competition among wage-earners for work, hampered and delayed as it is by frictions and elements of monopolistic policy, leads presently to the acceptance of lower money wages, whereas, on the other hand, when the percentage of unemployment is small, competition among employers for scarce labour tends to push money wages up. (Pigou, 1941, pp. 79–81)

The explicit expression of $\dot{w}$ as a function of the excess demand for labor seems to be due to Patinkin (1948, reprinted 1951):

let $N^s$ and $N^d$ be the amounts of labor supplied and demanded, respectively; $w$, the money wage rate; and $t$, time. Then a flexible dynamic system will, by definition, contain an equation of the general type

$$\frac{dw}{dt} = f(N^D - N^S)$$

where

$$\text{sign} \frac{dw}{dt} = \text{sign} (N^D - N^S).$$

If by equilibrium is meant a situation such that

$$\frac{dw}{dt} = 0$$

then clearly this system cannot be in equilibrium unless

$$(N^D - N^S) = 0$$

*i.e.*, unless there is full employment. (Patinkin, 1951, p. 279, footnote 13)

It may be that Keynes had in mind something like the wage indexation factor in the *Treatise*, chapter 11, p. 160, when he said, "There is another matter which deserves a word in passing. When for any reason on entrepreneur feels discouraged about the prospects, one or both of two courses may be open to him – he can reduce his output or he can reduce his costs by lowering his offers to the factors of production." Be that as it may, the inclusion of an explicit coefficient like our $\tau$ in the wage-adjustment function seems to have been the invention of Solow and Stiglitz, 1968 (p. 544, equation (9) ). But their multiplicand is the rate of inflation of *actual* prices, which in their model is not distinct from the rate of inflation of short-term normal prices. They also have a coefficient like our $\sigma$ in their equation (8) for the adjustment of actual prices, which is designed "to allow prices to be partially cost-determined, under some markup formula" (p. 543). The *expected* rate of inflation is omitted from both their adjustment functions.

The diametrical opposite of Keynes's case of full cost push is the special case of *full wage indexation*, in which $\tau$ is unity. Obviously in a system of differential equations which includes both (3.29) and (3.31) the two extreme cases are incompatible: movements of $w/p$ cannot be both exclusively determined by $x/v$ and exclusively determined by $Q^*$. Logic compels the assumption

$$\sigma\tau < 1. \tag{3.35}$$

### 3.3 Aggregative Dynamics: The Basic Construction

From the difficult task of gathering materials we now turn to the straightforward one of constructing from them a dynamic framework which will be general enough to accomodate a diverse assemblage of particular theories.

## The Dynamics of x

As $p$ and $w$ change in accordance with equations (3.29) and (3.31), the ratio of the demand for labor (in effiency units) to the stock of capital moves along the curve of marginal productivity at a rate determined by the elasticity of the curve and the rate at which the ratio of $p$ to $w$ is changing. From

$$f'(x) = w/p \tag{1.3}$$

we obtain, by differentiating with respect to time,

$$\dot{x}/x = \phi(x)(\dot{p}/p - \dot{w}/w), \tag{3.36}$$

where

$$\phi(x) = -f'(x)/xf''(x) > 0 \tag{3.37}$$

is the elasticity of that demand with respect to $w/p$.

## The Dynamics of v

We recall that

$$v = N^s/K \tag{1.5}$$

is the ratio of the supply of labor (in efficiency units) to the stock of capital. Substituting into its derivative with respect to time, viz. $\dot{v}/v = \dot{N}^s/N^s - \dot{K}/K$, the definition

$$\dot{N}^s/N^s = n \tag{3.38}$$

and the equation

$$\dot{K}/K = I^*(x, m, \lambda), \tag{3.16}$$

we obtain

$$\dot{v}/v = n - I^*(x, m, \lambda) \tag{3.39}$$

when the central bank's reserves are parametric to the temporary equilibrium.

## The Equations of Motion

The development of the temporary equilibrium with parametric reserves must obey the system of equations:

$$\dot{x}/x = aH[Q^*(x, m, \lambda)] - bF(x/v) \qquad (3.40)$$

$$\dot{p}/p - \lambda = cH[Q^*(x, m, \lambda)] + gF(x/v) \qquad (3.41)$$

$$\dot{w}/w - \lambda = hH[Q^*(x, m, \lambda)] + cF(x/v) \qquad (3.42)$$

$$\dot{v}/v = n - I^*(x, m, \lambda). \qquad (3.39)$$

The coefficients are as follows:

$$a = \phi(x)(1-\tau)/(1-\sigma\tau) \geq 0; \quad b = \phi(x)(1-\sigma)/(1-\sigma\tau) \geq 0;$$

$$c = 1/(1-\sigma\tau) > 0; \quad g = \sigma/(1-\sigma\tau) \geq 0; \quad h = \tau/(1-\sigma\tau) \geq 0. \,(3.43)$$

Equations (3.41) and (3.42) are the result of subtracting $\lambda$ from both (3.29) and (3.31), to obtain

$$\dot{p}/p - \lambda = H(Q^*) + \sigma(\dot{w}/w - \lambda) \qquad (3.44)$$

$$\dot{w}/w - \lambda = F(x/v) + \tau(\dot{p}/p - \lambda), \qquad (3.45)$$

and, by means of elimination, expressing both $\dot{p}/p - \lambda$ and $\dot{w}/w - \lambda$ as functions of $H$ and $F$ only. Then substitution of (3.44) and (3.45) into (3.36) yields equation (3.40).

For the development of the temporary equilibrium under Say's law the system must be modified by putting $Q^*=0$ always and replacing (3.39) by

$$\dot{v}/v = n - I^*(x) \qquad (3.46)$$

from (3.27).

In the remainder of this book we shall show that this system of equations constitutes a general framework within which, by various postulates concerning the behavior and significance of the free parameters, many macrodynamic theories can be fitted and brought into relation with one another.

**Notes**

1 The conclusion holds also in the Tobin-Solow case, where

$$r^*(x) = f(x) - xf'(x) \qquad (1.28)$$

and

$$I_x^* = S_x - S_r x f''(x). \qquad (3.28)'$$

# PART II

## Macrodynamics with a Constant Ratio of Available Factors

# 4

# Keynes's *General Theory*

In spite of the enormous literature on what Keynes really meant in his *General Theory* few subjects in the history of economic thought can have been approached with less regard for what the author actually said. Yet the evidence in the book itself and that which can be found in the *Collected Writings* provide enough material for a coherent statement of its essential characteristics. The purpose of this chapter is first to draw attention to aspects which seem not to have been clearly visible and, secondly, to place the theory in relation to our general system.

## 4.1 Temporary Equilibrium

In our exposition of Keynes's theory of interest we have taken for granted that, as in the *Treatise*, so also in the *General Theory*, the economy is always in a temporary equilibrium: the "instantaneous picture taken on the assumption of a given output" (1936, p. vii) was not discarded. Circumstantial evidence for this is provided by his letter to Hawtrey (Keynes, 1973b, p. 12), cited here in chapter 1, on the theory of interest, which was written after the publication of the *General Theory*. But there is direct evidence. Describing the working-out of the multiplier after an unforeseen increase in investment without any immediate change in the output of consumption-goods Keynes says:

In this event the efforts of those newly employed in the capital-goods industries to consume a proportion of their increased incomes will raise the prices of consumption-goods until a temporary equilibrium between demand and supply has been brought about partly by the high prices causing a postponement of consumption, partly by a redistribution of income in favour of the saving classes as an effect of the increased profits resulting from the higher prices, and partly by the higher prices causing a depletion of stocks. (Keynes, 1936, pp. 123–4)

## 4.2 Saving Equals Investment

From the equation for the money value of the excess demand for final output, deflated by $pK$,

$$X_g = I + C - f(x) - Q \tag{1.11}$$

it must be that in a temporary equilibrium

$$I^* + C^* = f(x) + Q^*, \tag{4.1}$$

that is, the sum of the values of planned investment and planned consumption equals total money income, which in turn is the sum of expected incomes and windfall profits. (These are all money values deflated by $pK$.)

One can define saving by deducting planned consumption either from *expected* income or from *actual* income. Let $S$ stand for the first alternative and $S'$ for the second. Then

$$S = f(x) - C, \tag{4.2}$$

and

$$S' = f(x) + Q - C. \tag{4.3}$$

In the temporary equilibrium, therefore,

$$S'^* = I^* = S^* + Q^*. \tag{4.4}$$

Since the economy is always in a temporary equilibrium, the first of the equations in (4.4) expresses what Keynes probably meant when he decided that saving and investment should be "so defined that they are necessarily equal in amount, being, for the community as a whole, merely different aspects of the same thing" (1936, p. 74). Unlike the second equation, which is equivalent to (4.1), it has no causal significance. With saving so defined it is necessary to go back to (4.1) to find the condition for equilibrium in the market for final output.

Clearness of mind on this matter is best reached, perhaps, by thinking in terms of decisions to consume (or to refrain from consuming) rather than of decisions to save. A decision to consume or not to consume truly lies within the power of the individual; so does a decision to invest or not to invest. The amounts of aggregate income and of aggregate saving are the *results* of the free choices of individuals whether or not to consume and whether or not to invest; but they are neither of them capable of assuming an independent value resulting from a separate set of decisions taken irrespective of the decisions concerning consumption and investment. In accordance with this principle, the conception of the *propensity to consume* will, in what follows, take the place of the propensity or disposition to save. (1936, p. 65)

Nevertheless $S'^* = I^*$ is not a mere truism. It is *not* equivalent to the national-income identity, "income less consumption equals investment," which is true even if the excess demand for final output is non-zero.

But of course the theory could have been set out just as clearly in terms of decisions to save as expressed by $S$. Why did Keynes reject this alternative? Perhaps it was because, according to the liquidity-preference theory of interest, $S^*$ has no significance in the market for loanable funds. It appeared, therefore, to be a redundant concept.

### 4.3 Expectations and Employment

There are three substantial differences between the *Treatise* and the *General Theory*. The first is a change from the classical to the Marshallian neoclassical conception of temporary equilibrium. The second is that a Marshallian short-period equilibrium of output and employment replaces the long-period equilibrium of the *Treatise* as the longer-run terminus *ad quem*. The third is that *changes* in output and employment are to be deduced by applying the method of comparative statics to the short-period equilibrium.

In the *Treatise* long-term expectations govern the employment of both capital and labor. But, as we showed in the Introduction, in the interval between the two books Keynes switched to the assumption that, while planned investment depends on long-term expectations, labor is variable in a shorter run than capital, and the demand for it depends on *short-term* expectations, that is, on the prices that are expected, at the outset of each instant, to emerge within it. The maximization of short-term expected profits then determines the instant's output and demand for labor on a given capital. And so it is in the *General Theory* itself:

Thus the behavior of each individual firm in deciding its daily[1] output will be determined by its *short-term expectations* – expectations as to the cost of output on various possible scales and expectations as to the sale-proceeds of this output . . . It is upon these various expectations that the amount of employment which the firms offer will depend. The *actually realised* results of the production and sale of output will only be relevant to employment in so far as they cause a modification of subsequent expectations. [1]*Daily* here stands for the shortest interval after which the firm is free to revise its decision as to how much employment to offer. It is, so to speak, the minimum effective unit of economic time. (1936, p. 47)

Comparing the new theory with his *Treatise on Money* Keynes says (1936, p. vii): "This book, on the other hand, has evolved into what is primarily a study of the forces which determine changes in the scale of output and employment as a whole." It was necessary, therefore, to assume that the temporary equilibrium converges rapidly to the short-period equilibrium. Changes in parameters such as the supply of the factors, the state of the arts, expected inflation, and the supply of deposits in terms of wage units, must be slow in comparison with the rate at which short-term expectations are modified. For this reason Keynes assumed for the most part that short-term expectations are always fulfilled. At the outset of each instant entrepreneurs, correctly anticipating the aggregate demand-price, choose the value of $x$ which will maximize their *actual* profit, $\pi^* f(x) - wx$, since $p = \pi^*$. This is the case of the instantaneous multiplier. The temporary equilibrium makes a quantum jump to the point of effective demand (where $x$ is such that actual money incomes coincide with short-term expectations of them). Indeed, by writing the book in such a way that the distinction between temporary and short-period equilibrium, though never abandoned, was pushed into the background, Keynes inadvertently originated the myth that he himself intended the temporary equilibrium and the *IS - LM* equilibrium to be one and the same.

Keynes did not, however, insist on correct short-term foresight. If short-term expectations are not always fulfilled, $p$ is adjusted by a process of trial and error from one instant to the next. Thus he says: "The fact that an unforeseen change only exercises its full effect on employment over a period of time is important in certain contexts – in particular it plays a part in the analysis of the trade cycle (on lines such as I followed in my *Treatise on Money*,") (1936, p. 124). As he explained in a letter to Hawtrey dated 8 November 1935 (Keynes, 1973a, pp. 602–3), correct short-term foresight seemed to be a justifiable short cut in the context of his short-period theory of employment:

In the passage you quote from p. 27 [of the book as published], as in many other passages, it is not relevant to my immediate purpose for me to super-impose the complication of entrepreneurs' making mistakes. It is, of course, quite true that in this passage I mean by the receipts of entre-preneurs the expected receipts. I am saying that in so far as employers have correct foresight, they will curtail the amount of employment they offer in accordance with the principle I state. But it really makes no difference if their foresight is momentarily incorrect, unless you are asserting a psychological law, that employers are chronically subject to a particular type of false expectation which leads them, in the contingency I am contemplating, to fail to curtail employment to the proper level, and hence habitually to make a loss . . . For, it would all come to exactly the same thing if one were to suppose that the decisions of employers were not brought about by any rational attempt to foresee on the lines I indicate, but merely functioned by modifications at short intervals solely based on the method of trial and error. For, the method of trial and error would lead to exactly the same results.

His position, then, was that, while correct short-term foresight and (sufficiently rapid) modification of short-term expectations by trial and error lead to the same results in the short-period theory of employment, in other contexts, such as the analysis of business cycles, it will be important to attend to the consequences of less rapid reactions to unforeseen changes.

Later, in a set of rough notes from his 1937 lectures (Keynes, 1973b, p. 181), he expressed the wish that he had made more of the method of trial and error in the *General Theory* itself: "I now feel that if I were writing the book again I should begin by setting forth my theory on the assumption that short-period expectations were always fulfilled; and then have a subsequent chapter showing what difference it makes when short-period expectations are disappointed."

### 4.4 Money-wage Flexibility and Employment

The *General Theory* was erected on three pillars. One of them was the new concept of short-period equilibrium. The other two were imported from the *Treatise on Money*. They were the liquidity-preference theory of interest and the conviction that perfect flexibility of *money* wages would not ensure perfect flexibility of *real* wages.

There is no need to repeat here what we have said about the meaning of the liquidity-preference theory and its significance in Keynes's attack on Say's law and the "classical" theory of interest. Let us consider, then, his objection to the idea that full employment would result from perfect flexibility of money wages, regardless of the kind of monetary policy in effect.

Both the fact of Keynes's objection to the efficacy of money-wage flexibility and apparently the only reason he ever gave for it are contained in the following extracts.

The traditional theory maintains, in short, *that the wage bargains between the entrepreneurs and the workers determine the real wage*; so that, assuming free competition amongst employers and no restrictive combination amongst workers, the latter can, if they wish, bring their real wages into conformity with the marginal disutility of the amount of employment offered by the employers at that wage . . . Now this assumption . . . is far from being consistent with the general tenor of the classical theory, which has taught us to believe that prices are governed by marginal prime cost in terms of money and that money-wages largely govern marginal prime cost. Thus if money-wages change, one would have expected the classical school to argue that prices would change in almost the same proportion, leaving the real wage and the level of unemployment practically the same as before, any small gain or loss to labour being at the expense or profit of other elements of marginal cost which have been left unaltered.[1] . . . There may exist no expedient by which labour as a whole can reduce its *real* wage to a given figure by making revised *money* bargains with the entrepreneurs. This will be our contention. (1936, pp. 10–13)

[1]This argument would, indeed, contain, to my thinking, a large element of truth, though the complete results of a change in money-wages are more complex, as we shall show in Chapter 19 below.

The "reason" is simply a restatement of the claim which he had made in the *Treatise*, and which he apparently found self-evident, that changes in money wages, except in so far as they have the *indirect* effect of changing the aggregate demand for goods, leave unchanged the real wage on which the demand for labor depends. It is expressed by the hypothesis that in our equation (3.40) $b=0$ because $\sigma=1$.

One seeks in vain for an argument to support this claim even in his chapter 19. All I can find is this (p. 261): "Perhaps it will help to rebut the crude conclusion that a reduction in money-wages will increase employment 'because it reduces the cost of production', if we follow up the course of events on the hypothesis most favourable to this view, namely that at the outset entrepreneurs *expect* the reduction in money-wages to have this effect," and so increase their output. But if the short-period equilibrium is stable, "the proceeds realised from the increased output will disappoint the entrepreneurs and employment will fall back again to its previous figure," unless the reduction in money wages increases the aggregate demand for output (p. 262).

But the fact that a *once-for-all* reduction in money wages need have no lasting effect on output and employment is irrelevant to the question of the efficacy of *money-wage flexibility* which Keynes proposed for discussion in chapter 19, the question whether it is valid, "to rest the supposedly self-adjusting character of the economic system on an assumed fluidity of money-wages; and, when there is rigidity, to lay on this rigidity the blame of maladjustment" (p. 257).

### 4.5 The Passage to Short-period Equilibrium

Let us now try to place Keynes's short-period equilibrium, and the passage to it through trial-and-error revisions of short-term expectations, in relation to our general system.

In the first place, since factor supplies and the state of the arts do not change significantly, the changes in

$$v=N^s/K, \tag{1.5}$$

the ratio of the supply of efficiency-labor to the stock of capital, governed by the equation

$$\dot{v}/v=n-I^*(x, m, \lambda), \tag{3.39}$$

must be ignored. In short-period analysis $v$ is a constant,

$$v = \bar{v}, \tag{4.5}$$

say.

Secondly, since money-wage flexibility has no direct effect on the demand for labor, it must be assumed that $\sigma = 1$, so that

$$b = 0 \tag{4.6}$$

in (3.40) and

$$g = c \tag{4.7}$$

in (3.41).

Thirdly, since the supply of real balances in terms of wage units is one of the parameters of the short-period equilibrium, we shall eliminate $m$ in favor of $z$ by means of

$$R/k = m = zf'(x). \tag{3.1}$$

(We recall that in the temporary equilibrium with $\alpha = 0$ the potential supply of real balances is also the actual supply.)

From these ingredients we obtain from our general system the equations

$$\dot{x}/x = aH[Q^*(x, zf'(x), \lambda)] \tag{4.8}$$

$$\dot{p}/p - \lambda = c[H(Q^*) + F(x/\bar{v})] \tag{4.9}$$

$$\dot{w}/w - \lambda = hH(Q^*) + cF(x/\bar{v}). \tag{4.10}$$

Before outlining the theory of employment in chapter 3, section II, Keynes says (p. 27): "In this summary we shall assume that the money-wage and other factor costs are constant per unit of labour employed. But this simplification, with which we shall dispense later, is introduced solely to facilitate the exposition. The essential character of the argument is precisely the same whether or not money-wages, etc., are liable to change." So far as the passage to the short-period equilibrium is concerned that is true, provided that the adjustment of short-term expectations is rapid in relation not only to changes in $v$ but also to changes in $z$ and $\lambda$, so that these parameters of the temporary equilibrium stay put during the adjustment. For then one can regard equation (4.8) as an autonomous differential equation in $x$ alone, without assuming either that $z$ and $\lambda$ are actually constant or that they have no effect on $Q^*$.

In a short-period equilibrium with "involuntary" unemployment the temporary-equilibrium equations have become

$$I(0, r^*; x^*) = S(0, r^*; x^*) \tag{4.11}$$

$$L(0, r^*; x^*, \lambda) = z f'(x^*) \tag{4.12}$$

$$\pi^* = p^* = w/f'(x^*), \tag{4.13}$$

with

$$x^* < \bar{v}. \tag{4.14}$$

This is, of course, the *IS–LM* equilibrium. $r^*$ and $x^*$ are such that planned saving equals investment and the demand for deposits in terms of wage units equals the supply.

The equilibrium is unique and stable if

$$\frac{dQ^*}{dx} = Q_x^* + Q_m^* z f''(x) < 0 \tag{4.15}$$

for all $x$. Substituting for $Q_x^*$ and $Q_m^*$ from (3.6) and (3.7), with $\alpha = 0$ in the expression $\Delta$, we find that

$$\frac{dQ^*}{dx} = \frac{(I_r - S_r) L_x - L_r (I_x - S_x) - (I_r - S_r) z f''(x)}{(I_Q - S_Q - 1) L_r - L_Q (I_r - S_r)} \tag{4.16}$$

Therefore, if $I_r - S_r$ is negative, the condition is that the gradient of the *LM* curve exceeds that of the *IS* curve; while if $I_r - S_r$ is zero, it is that the marginal inducement to invest is less than the marginal propensity to save.

But Keynes did, surely, need to assume that in the *IS–LM* equilibrium itself money-wage flexibility is zero when there is less than full employment: that, when $x^*$ is less than $\bar{v}$,

$$F(x^*/\bar{v}) = 0, \tag{4.17}$$

in order to get rid of the persistent error about expected inflation that is otherwise implied by the equations

$$(\dot{p}/p)^* - \lambda = (\dot{w}/w)^* - \lambda = cF(x^*/\bar{v}), \tag{4.18}$$

which follow from (4.9) and (4.10) when $Q^*$ is zero. He likewise needed to assume that both expected inflation and the supply of real balances in terms of wage units, which are parameters of the temporary equilibrium, are also parameters of the *IS–LM* equilibrium,

$$\lambda = \bar{\lambda} \tag{4.19}$$

$$z = \bar{z}. \tag{4.20}$$

If these assumptions are not made, the significance of exercises in comparative statics, intended to predict changes in output and employment, is impaired by the fact that the equilibrium may be shifting under the influence of unrecorded dynamic forces.

### 4.6 The Relation of Aggregate Demand to Short-period Employment

The *General Theory* opens with an attack on the postulates of the "classical" theory, whereby it is supposed to have ruled out "involuntary" unemployment due to deficiency of the aggregate demand for output. They are (1) that money-wage flexibility has a direct effect on the demand for labor (pp. 11–13); and (2) that supply creates its own demand (pp. 18–21); so that, if money wages are not altogether inflexible, the real wage will clear the labor market.

Assume that, because of Say's law, $Q^*$ is zero for all values of $x$ and $\lambda$. In conjunction with the short-period assumption (4.5) equations (3.40), (3.41) and (3.42) reduce respectively to

$$\dot{x}/x = -bF(x/\bar{v}) \tag{4.21}$$

$$\dot{p}/p - \lambda = gF(x/\bar{v}) \tag{4.22}$$

$$\dot{w}/w - \lambda = cF(x/\bar{v}). \tag{4.23}$$

If $b$ is positive and $F(x/\bar{v})$ is strictly increasing, the economy converges to a short-period equilibrium in which the labor market is cleared ($x^* = \bar{v}$), and both $p$ and $w$ are changing at the rate $\lambda$. (The theory has nothing to say about the magnitude of $\lambda$ itself.)

It is impossible, however, to make sense of Keynes's claim, at the end of chapter 2, that Say's law on its own is enough to guarantee full employment. It seems to be based on a logical error. For in chapter 3 he says that, if supply creates its own demand,

effective demand, instead of having a unique equilibrium value, is an infinite range of values all equally admissible; and the amount of employment is indeterminate except in so far as the marginal disutility of labour sets an upper limit. If this were true, competition between entrepreneurs would always lead to an expansion of employment up to the point at which the supply of output as a whole ceases to be elastic, *i.e.* where a further increase in the value of the effective demand will no longer be accompanied by an increase in output. Evidently this amounts to the same thing as full employment. (Keynes, 1936, p. 26)

If, as he believed, $b$ is zero, then certainly (4.21) entails that $x$ is indeterminate in the sense that there is no force tending to change it, just as there is no force tending to change it if money wages are perfectly inflexible (that is, if $F(x/\bar{v})$ is zero). The real wage is stuck at its initial value. However, his conclusion, that in these circumstances competition between entrepreneurs would establish full employment, is simply a non-sequitur. Hawtrey pointed this out to him in a letter dated 15 April 1936:

You interpret the principle, "supply creates its own demand", to mean that $'f(n)$ and $\phi(n)$ are equal for *all* values of $N'$. That is to say, if the entrepreneurs are in fact employing $N$ men, the aggregate of the proceeds they expect is equal to the aggregate of the proceeds which will just make it worth while to employ $N$ men. You infer that competition between entrepreneurs would always lead to an expansion of employment up to the limit of full employment. The argument here is not at all clear. You say on page 25 that "if $D$ is greater than $Z$ there will be an incentive to entrepreneurs to increase employment beyond $N$". But if $D$ is equal to $Z$ why should there be any tendency to change? Or why should the change be an increase rather than a decrease? (Keynes, 1973b, pp. 31–2)

The proper conclusion, which is not without interest, is that an economy with full cost push is like an economy with perfectly inflexible money wages; it cannot function under Say's law.

Perhaps it is worth completing the account of the relation between aggregate demand and employment with the observation that there are, theoretically, two cases in which the aggregate demand for output cannot affect the demand for labor. One is Say's law. The other is full wage indexation, in which $a=0$ because $\tau=1$. Under this hypothesis the equations of motion for the short period become

$$\dot{x}/x = -bF(x/\bar{v}) \tag{4.21}$$

$$\dot{p}/p - \lambda = cH[Q^*(x, zf'(x), \lambda] + gF(x/\bar{v}) \tag{4.24}$$

$$\dot{w}/w - \lambda = hH[Q^*(x, zf'(x), \lambda)] + cF(x/\bar{v}), \tag{4.25}$$

where, by (3.43), $b=\phi(x)$ and $h=c$. Since $b$ must be positive, there is convergence to equilibrium in the labor market provided that money wages are not wholly inflexible, just as in the Say's-law case when $b$ is positive. But aggregate demand does affect inflation. Therefore, whereas under Say's law inflation is indeterminate, full wage indexation would offer a painless means of manipulating it through monetary policy.

# 5

# Demand-determined Growth, Employment, and Fluctuations

## 5.1 A Constant Factor Supply Ratio: Two Interpretations

For short-period analysis it is necessary to replace the differential equation

$$\dot{v}/v = n - I^*(x, m, \lambda) \tag{3.39}$$

by the hypothesis that $v = N^s/K$ is a constant,

$$v = \bar{v}. \tag{4.5}$$

But there is a longer-run interpretation of (4.5), namely that at all times $n$, the sum of the growth rates of the work force and efficiency per unit of labor, equals the growth rate of capital:

$$n = I^*(x, m, \lambda), \tag{5.1}$$

because the growth of efficiency per unit of labor through labor-augmenting technical change is determined by, and equal to, the growth of capital per unit of labor supplied. Consequently any theory of the short period is formally equivalent to a theory of the long period with a constant ratio of available factors, $\bar{v}$.

Such theories, which are the subject matter of this Part, are quite different from those dealt with in Part III, in which $v$ is a variable, governed by equation (3.39), and $n$ is a constant, the exogenously given "natural" rate of growth. If $n$ is at all times equal to $I^*$, there is no unique natural rate of growth: every growth rate of the stock of capital is a natural rate, equal to the growth rate of $N^s$ which it determines endogenously.

## 5.2 Expansion and Employment: Domar's Theory

Domar (1946, reprinted 1957) seems to have based his theory of expansion and employment on this assumption that technological change is such as to keep $v$ constant, or at least approximately constant. Introducing his theory, he says (1957, p. 72): "As Mrs. Robinson well remarked, 'The rate of increase in productivity of labor is not something given by Nature.' Labor productivity is not a function of technological progress in the abstract, but technological progress embodied in capital goods, and the amount of capital goods in general." Also in his later reflections on it (1957, p. 7) he tells us that he had fashioned it "in the hope that technological progress and the growth of population would provide a sufficient labor force to man the new plants without denuding the old."

Domar uses this assumption to release Keynes's unemployment equilibrium from its confinement to the short period. But the result would not be very convincing if there were a monetary policy for full-employment equilibrium. The same obstacle stands in the way of any other long-period generalization of the *General Theory*. It is not surprising, therefore, to find that Keynes's successors were typically extreme Keynesians, believing that monetary policy is ineffective.

Domar made the economy move to an equilibrium of steady growth in which both the rate of expansion and the ratio of total output to productive capacity are determined by effective demand. The *productive capacity* of an economy is "its total output when its labor force is fully employed in some conventional sense" (p. 71). Presumably, then, he would have found acceptable the convention that productive capacity means *normal capacity*, which we define as total output when unemployment equals unfilled vacancies.

If $P$ is productive capacity in this sense, we have

$$P=Kf(\bar{v}), \tag{5.2}$$

where $f(\bar{v})$ is Domar's "ratio of productive capacity to capital for the whole economy" (p. 76), which he calls $s$. But there is a difficulty at this point. For he draws a distinction between $s$ and "the *potential social average investment productivity*," which is the ratio of the *rate of increase* in productive capacity to the *rate of investment*. The latter ratio is $\sigma=\dot{P}/\dot{K}$, and he says (p. 74): "$s$ is the maximum that $\sigma$ can attain. The difference between them will depend on the magnitude of the rate of investment on the one hand, and on the growth of other factors, such as labor and natural resources, and on technological progress on the other. A misdirection of investment will also produce a difference between $s$ and $\sigma$."

This passage casts some doubt on his commitment to the assumption that $v$ is strictly constant. But, since he does not explain how an excess of $s$ over $\sigma$ is formally related to changes in $v$, we are forced to limit our exposition of his theory to the only case in which it is clear-cut, namely "the special simple case $\sigma = s$" (p. 76).

Under this limitation the essence of the theory can be distilled by combining the long-period interpretation of $\bar{v}$ with an extreme Keynesian specialization of our general system. We assume that

$$I_r = S_r = 0 \tag{5.3}$$

and

$$F(x/v) = 0. \tag{5.4}$$

From (1.23), (1.25), (1.27), (3.1), (3.16), (5.3), and (5.4) the equations for the extreme-Keynesian temporary equilibrium are

$$Q^* = I(Q^*; x, \xi) - S(Q^*; x) \tag{5.5}$$

$$L(Q^*, r^*; x, \lambda) = z f'(x) \tag{5.6}$$

$$\pi^* = p + p Q^* / f(x) \tag{5.7}$$

$$\dot{K}/K = I(Q^*; x, \xi). \tag{5.8}$$

The parameter $\xi$ which we have put into the planned-investment function stands for the state of long-term expectations in so far as it is independent of short-term expectations, and by convention

$$I_\xi > 0. \tag{5.9}$$

We may say that "autonomous" and "induced" changes in investment are caused respectively by changes in $\xi$ and changes in $x$.

Using (4.8), (4.9), and (4.10) we obtain the dynamic equations

$$\dot{x}/x = a H[Q^*(x, \xi)] \tag{5.10}$$

$$\dot{p}/p - \lambda = c H(Q^*) \tag{5.11}$$

$$\dot{w}/w - \lambda = h H(Q^*). \tag{5.12}$$

Since $Q^*_m$ and $Q^*_\lambda$ are always zero on account of (5.3), (3.7) and (3.8), we have written $Q^*(x, \xi)$ for $Q^*(x, m, \lambda, \xi)$.

When the temporary equilibrium is consistent with a long-period equilibrium of steady growth, its equations are

$$I(0; x^*, \xi) = S(0; x^*) \tag{5.13}$$

$$L(0, r^*; x^*, \lambda) = zf'(x^*) \tag{5.14}$$

$$\dot{K}/K = I(0; x^*, \xi) \tag{5.15}$$

$$\pi^* = p^* = w/f'(x^*), \tag{4.13}$$

with

$$(\dot{w}/w)^* = \lambda, \tag{5.16}$$

from (5.12).

The equality of planned saving and investment in (5.13) determines $x^*$. The equilibrium rate of growth follows from (5.15). The price levels and their equilibrium rate of inflation ($\lambda$) are indeterminate. The general level of interest rates satisfies (5.14), but it will be constant only if both $\lambda$ and the supply of real balances in terms of wage units ($z$) is constant. However, its behavior is of no consequence.

The long-period equilibrium value of $x$ is unique and asymptotically stable if the marginal inducement to invest ($I_x$) is less than the marginal propensity to save ($S_x$) for all $x$.

In the long-period equilibrium both the *level* of investment ($KI$) and the stock of capital will be growing at the same constant percentage rate, for which Domar uses the symbol $r$ (1957, p. 76). He proceeds, under simplifying assumptions, to derive formulae (p. 77):

1  for the value which this growth rate $r$ (not to be confused with our complex of interest rates!) must have if there is to be continuous full employment, and
2  for the ratio of total output to productive capacity when $r$ is below this value.

Suppose that the marginal inducement to invest is zero and the proportion of income saved is constant, so that equations (5.13) and (5.15) become

$$I(0; \xi) = r = \alpha f(x^*) = \dot{K}/K, \tag{5.17}$$

where $\alpha$ is the saving ratio in Domar's notation. Then

1  there will be full employment in the long-period equilibrium if and only if the value of $\xi$ is such that

$$r = \alpha f(\bar{v}) = \alpha \sigma, \tag{5.18}$$

but

2 if $\xi$ is less than this, since total output is

$$Y = K f(x) \tag{5.19}$$

and $f(x^*) = r/\alpha$ by (5.17), Domar's *"coefficient of utilization"* of productive capacity

$$Y^*/P = f(x^*)/f(\bar{v}) = r/\alpha f(\bar{v}) = r/\alpha \sigma \tag{5.20}$$

is less than unity.

## 5.3 Domar and Harrod

There is a resemblance between Domar's formula $r = \alpha \sigma$ for "the equilibrium [sc. full-employment] rate of growth" (1957, p. 75) and one of Harrod's formulae for his "warranted rate of growth", viz. $G_w = s/C_r$ (see Harrod, 1948, p. 81). Harrod's $s$ is the same as Domar's $\alpha$, and his $C_r$ stands for "the requirement for new capital divided by the increment of output to sustain which the new capital is required" (p. 82). This, together with the fact that both authors were extending extreme Keynesian ideas to the long period, led many people to believe that their views were essentially the same.

But if we have delineated Domar' theory with fair accuracy, the resemblance is illusory. For, first, all of Harrod's several formulae for the warranted rate are derived from the acceleration principle, which does not appear in Domar. Harrod's "required" new capital is, at least in part, justified by the growth of output. Secondly, growth at a warranted rate does not imply full employment. Thirdly, he contrasts it sharply with growth at the natural rate. These points are made in the following extracts:

$G_w$ is the entrepreneurial equilibrium; it is the line of advance, which, if achieved, will satisfy profit takers that they have done the right thing; in Keynesian fashion it contemplates the possibility of growing "involuntary" unemployment. (Harrod, 1939, p. 87)

Warranted and natural rates of growth are entirely different concepts, and they have different determinants. The warranted rate is that at which desired saving is equal to required investment . . . a substantial part of investment is a direct function of the growth rate, being needed to sustain increments of production . . . The determinants of the natural rate are, by contrast, the increase in the population of working age and the nature of current technological progress. (Harrod, 1973, p. 100)

In fact, since our $v$ is *not* a constant in Harrod's scheme of things, his ideas properly belong in Part III.

### 5.4 Business Cycles and Economic Growth: Duesenberry and Robinson

The fluctuations which we call business cycles have typically been around a growing trend. But they have differed in their amplitude and periodicity at different times and places. With these two facts in mind Duesenberry set up a model for a theory with the following general characteristics (see Duesenberry, 1958, and in particular, his summary on pp. 275–6).

1 There is a demand-determined stable trend rate of constant growth, and associated with it a trend ratio of capital to output.
2 Most downswings are in response to temporary exogenous disturbances, especially to temporary declines in autonomous investment (pp. 249–52), which reduce the stable trend rate of growth.
3 But "eventually the investment demand function will shift upward again because of the elimination of the original cause of the downward shift" (p. 276).
4 The amplitude and duration of the cycle are governed by the size and duration of the temporary disturbance, and by the strength of the forces which first draw the economy towards the reduced rate of growth and then draw it back again to the original rate after the recovery of autonomous investment.
5 But there may also be a smaller constant rate of growth, and associated with it a larger trend value of $K/Y$, which is unstable. Therefore a large downward disturbance of long duration may carry the economy below its low-level unstable trend rate of growth, causing a major depression: "the upward shift in investment demand may produce a recovery, but whether it will or not depends on how much increase in the ratio of capital to income has taken place as well as on sensitivity of saving and investment to increases in the capital-income ratio" (p. 276).

But recovery from such a depression presents a problem which Duesenberry does not solve. Clearly a supplementary theory would be needed to provide for an eventual upturn.

Duesenberry's argument is couched in terms of a two-dimensional homogenous system of difference equations in $Y$ and $K$, with constant coefficients. We are always in a short-period extreme Keynesian equilibrium. But, because of lags, today's output and investment are determined by yesterday's output and capital. Hence his pair of difference equations (4c) and (3c) on p. 196.

It is assumed that the eigenvalues of the system's coefficient matrix are real, and that at least one of them is positive. The larger eigenvalue is the stable rate of growth, and its corresponding eigenvector determines the stable value of $K/Y$. Suppose that the smaller eigenvalue is also positive. Then if $K/Y$ is initially below the critical level associated with the smaller eigenvalue, the economy will tend towards the larger rate of growth, but if it is initially above the critical level, the economy will go into a progressive decline. Temporary disturbances of the elements in the coefficient matrix reduce the magnitude of the stable growth rate, causing $K/Y$ to rise. Recovery occurs only if the disturbance is removed before $K/Y$ has risen above the critical level. It is not, however, necessary that this critical level should exist; for the smaller eigenvalue may be negative.

Whatever views one may have of the theory summarized in propositions (1)–(5), a simpler, and I think happier, mode of expressing it is in the setting of the model in section 5.2. Happier both because its rates of steady growth become economically meaningful equilibria and because its relation to other macro-dynamic theories is more easily grasped.

Take, first, the case of an economy in a long-period growth equilibrium which is unique and stable. A temporary fall in $\xi$ reduces it. Aggregate windfall losses are made at the old equilibrium value of $x$. There is consequently a downswing towards the new stable equilibrium as short-term expectations sag. But in due course the (assumed) recovery of $\xi$ restores the original equilibrium, and the economy returns to its "normal" steady state under the influence of aggregate windfall profits.

It must be confessed that it is rather difficult to justify on economic grounds the existence of a second, unstable equilibrium at a lower rate of growth. Perhaps there are diminishing returns to basing long-term expectations on short-term expected profits $f(x) - xf'(x)$ as the latter increase, so that $I_{xx}$ is negative. If so, the curve depicting $I(0; x, \xi)$ as a function of $x$ at a "normal" value of $\xi$ could intersect the curve depicting $S(0; x)$ twice, with $I_x > S_x$ at the lower intersection and $I_x < S_x$ at the higher.

In this second case with two equilibria a horror story could be told of a prolonged fall in $\xi$ carrying the $I$ curve wholly below the $S$ curve, causing both equilibria to disappear until $x$ had fallen below the low-level equilibrium associated with the "normal" value of $\xi$. The mere restoration of $\xi$ to its "normal" value would not be enough for recovery, even if such a resurgence of optimism were likely in the circumstances.

Robinson (1962, Essay II) has a similar model for Duesenberry's type of theory. She calls the unstable equilibrium the economy's "stalling speed" (p. 49). There is, however, a difference between our dynamics and hers. Since her economy is always in a short-period equilibrium (pp. 46-7) in which planned saving is equal to investment, the movements of the economy when it is not in a long-period equilibrium cannot be in response to the net sum of windfall profits; for in the short-period equilibrium the sum is zero. Another lag is called for. She finds it (pp. 48-9) in Kalecki's postulate (Kalecki, 1937, pp. 82-3) that the current rate of accumulation has been determined by decisions taken in the past – not only capital but also investment is "quasi-fixed" – and that there is a rate of accumulation justified by current profit-expectations, let us call it $J(x, \xi)$, such that the actual rate of accumulation $I$ increases or decreases according to whether $J$ is greater or less than $I$. Therefore the equation for $\dot{x}$ can be deduced from the equations

$$S(0; x) = I \tag{5.21}$$

$$\dot{I} = \epsilon [J(x, \xi) - I], \tag{5.22}$$

where $\epsilon$ is a positive coefficient of adjustment. It is

$$\dot{x} = (\epsilon / S_x) \cdot [J(x, \xi) - S(0; x)]. \tag{5.23}$$

If $J_x$ is positive and $J_{xx}$ is negative, there may be two long-period equilibrium rates of growth. The larger rate is asymptotically stable if in its neighborhood $J_x < S_x$. At the smaller rate, which is the economy's stalling speed, the inequality is reversed.

When a fall in $\xi$ reduces the stable equilibrium, the rate of accumulation declines in accordance with (5.22). Planned saving also declines (equation 5.21), and with it so does $x$ via Keynes's instantaneous multiplier; for the marginal propensity to save is positive. But if the equilibrium is stable, the decline in $x$ reduces the gap between justified investment and actual saving-investment.

In Robinson's model "the rate of profit" takes the place of our $x$ as the argument both in the planned-saving function (1962, pp. 38–9) and in the justified-investment function (p. 48). That makes no essential difference to the dynamic theory, however, provided that both planned saving and justified investment are increasing functions of the rate of profit, and that the second derivative of justified investment with respect to the rate of profit is negative.

# 6

# Normal-capacity Equilibrium and Monetary Dynamics

## 6.1 Normal-capacity Equilibrium

Even if business cycles are "the alternation of expansions and contractions around a rising trend" (Haberler, 1963, p. viii), it may be deemed reasonable to provide for the alternation from outside, as in Duesenberry's type of theory. Matthews, for example, in his review of Duesenberry's book, was of the opinion that "in the nature of things the shock is likely to reverse itself presently" (Matthews, 1959, p. 760). But those with less confidence in this aspect of the nature of things have preferred that the alternation should be an intrinsic property of the solutions to a dynamic system. For this purpose a system of at least the second order is normally required.

In this chapter we consider various ways of closing the general open-ended system

$$\dot{x}/x = aH[Q^*(x, m, \lambda)] - bF(x/\bar{v}) \tag{6.1}$$

$$\dot{p}/p - \lambda = cH[Q^*(x, m, \lambda)] + gF(x/\bar{v}) \tag{6.2}$$

$$\dot{w}/w - \lambda = hH[Q^*(x, m, \lambda)] + cF(x/\bar{v}) \tag{6.3}$$

implied by (3.40), (3.41). and (3.42) with

$$v = \bar{v} \tag{4.5}$$

in place of (3.39), when the extreme-Keynesian position expressed by (5.3) and (5.4) is replaced by the assumptions that $Q_m^*$ is positive ($I_r < S_r$) and $F(x/v)$ is strictly increasing.

For ease of reference we repeat here the equations of the temporary equilibrium on which these forces act. They are:

$$Q^* = I(Q^*, r^*; x) - S(Q^*, r^*, x) \tag{1.23}$$

$$\alpha Q^* = \gamma [m - L(Q^*, r^*; x, \lambda)], \tag{3.2}$$

$$\pi^* = p + pQ^*/f(x). \tag{1.29}$$

$$\dot{K}/K = I(Q^*, r^*; x). \tag{3.17}$$

$$f'(x) = w/p. \tag{1.3}$$

We shall arrange that, when the dynamic system has been completed by postulates governing the behavior of $m$ and $\lambda$, among its solutions there will be a *normal-capacity equilibrium*, defined as a steady state $(x^*, m^*, \lambda^*)$ in which aggregate windfalls are zero $(Q^* = 0)$ and output is at normal capacity $(x^* = \bar{v})$. Evidently one is free to choose between a short-period and a long-period interpretation, but in either case it is obvious that in such an equilibrium

$$\dot{\pi}^*/\pi^* = (\dot{p}/p)^* = (\dot{w}/w)^* = \lambda^*. \tag{6.4}$$

The second and third equations in (6.4) are the result of putting $Q^* = 0$ and $x^* = \bar{v}$ in (6.2) and (6.3), because $H(0) = F(1) = 0$. The first equation then follows from (1.29); for $Q^* = 0 \Leftrightarrow \pi^* = p$.

But the converse is also true: if a steady state has $\dot{x} = 0$ and $\dot{p}/p = \lambda$, then it is a normal-capacity equilibrium.

*Proof*   The matrix equation implied by (6.1) and (6.2) when $\dot{x} = 0$ and $\dot{p}/p = \lambda$, namely

$$\begin{bmatrix} a & -b \\ c & g \end{bmatrix} \begin{bmatrix} H \\ F \end{bmatrix} = \begin{bmatrix} 0 \\ 0 \end{bmatrix}, \tag{6.5}$$

has only the trivial solution $H = F = 0$, because the coefficient matrix is non-singular. For from (3.35), (3.37), and (3.43) its determinant

$$ag + bc = \phi(x)/(1 - \sigma\tau) > 0. \tag{6.6}$$

Similarly, a steady state is a normal-capacity equilibrium if it has $\dot{x} = 0$ and $\dot{w}/w = \lambda$, because $ac + hg$ is also equal to $\phi(x)/(1 - \sigma\tau)$.

## 6.2 Cycles of Prices and Employment

One way of closing the system is by means of the following two assumptions:

*Assumption (6.1)*

The expected inflation of short-term normal prices $\lambda$ is a constant, but its magnitude is such that it will be realized in the longer-run equilibrium.

*Assumption (6.2)*

At the outset of each instant the central bank chooses the ratio of the potential nominal supply of deposits to the stock of capital, normally changing it from one instant to the next at a constant percentage rate, with the idea of determining a constant average rate of inflation or deflation.

The main point of Assumption (6.1) is simplification. But it also helps to justify the central bank's monetary policy, inasmuch as such a policy runs the risk of being ineffectual when expected inflation is adaptive.

*The Model*

Let

$$M = pKm \tag{6.7}$$

be the potential nominal supply of deposits. If $\mu$ is the constant percentage rate of change of $M/K$ that the central bank normally brings about from one instant to the next, Assumption (6.2) is that

$$M/K = \rho e^{\mu t}, \tag{6.8}$$

where $\rho > 0$ and $\mu$ are parameters. Therefore,

$$\dot{M}/M - \dot{K}/K = \mu. \tag{6.9}$$

(Under the short-period interpretation of the model $\dot{K}$ is assumed to be negligible). Differentiating (6.7) with respect to time and substituting from (6.9), we obtain

$$\dot{m}/m = \mu - \dot{p}/p, \tag{6.10}$$

so that

$$\dot{m}/m = \mu - \lambda - cH[Q^*(x, m, \lambda)] - gF(x/\bar{v}) \tag{6.11}$$

from (6.2).

Since $\lambda$ is a constant by Assumption (6.1), equations (6.1) and (6.11) constitute a second-order autonomous system in $x$ and $m$. But by the same Assumption and equation (6.10) it must be the case that

$$\lambda = \lambda^* = \mu. \tag{6.12}$$

Otherwise $\dot{x} = \dot{m} = 0 \Rightarrow (\dot{p}/p)^* = \mu \neq \lambda^*$. Consequently the second-order system implied by Assumptions (6.1) and (6.2) is

$$\dot{x} = x\{aH[Q^*(x, m, \mu)] - bF(x/\bar{v})\} \tag{6.13}$$

$$\dot{m} = -m\{cH[Q^*(x, m, \mu)] + gF(x/\bar{v})\}. \tag{6.14}$$

This is a model for two different theories of monetary cycles. One of them has cumulative upswings and downswings of output and employment, relative to normal capacity, which are reversed by the onset of tight and easy money (high and low rates of interest) respectively. In this regard it resembles a theory expressed verbally by Hawtrey (1926, reprinted 1944), which Haberler (1963, ch. 2) calls "the purely monetary theory" of cycles, presumably to contrast it with "the over-investment theories" (1963, chs 3, 4), in which movements of the stock of capital (changes in our $v$) are of central importance.

In the other theory there are no such cumulative upswings and downswings; for the onset of tight and easy money prevents them. But the tightening (easing) of money, which continues after the employment percentage has begun to fall (rise), is strong enough to cause the percentage to overshoot its equilibrium. This theory is implicit in a model constructed by A. W. Phillips (1961).

We shall show that there is a special case of our model which can produce cycles of this sort. But Phillips's model does not encompass both kinds of cycles. The question why this is so is sufficiently interesting to warrant a comparison of his model with ours.

There is another special case which, though interesting in itself, will be excluded from further consideration because it renders the model incapable of producing business cycles. It is the case mentioned at the end of chapter 4, where $\tau$ is unity (full wage indexation). The properties of the model with this specialization are virtually the same as those of Tobin's "$M$-Model" (Tobin, 1975, pp. 199–200).[1] Since $a$ is zero, aggregate demand affects prices but not employment, and movements of real efficiency wages induced by disequilibrium in the labor market cause $x$ to approach $\bar{v}$ monotonically.

## The Equilibrium

The proof given in section 6.1 tells us that a steady state of this system must be a normal-capacity equilibrium. It can be obtained by first adjoining to the temporary-equilibrium equations the definition of $M$ in (6.7), the monetary policy specified (6.8) and the value of $\lambda$ in (6.12), and then setting $Q^*=0$ and $x=\bar{v}$. The complete set of equilibrium relations is:

$$Q^* = 0 \tag{6.15}$$

$$x^* = \bar{v} \tag{6.16}$$

$$I(0, r^*; \bar{v}) = S(0, r^*; \bar{v}) \tag{6.17}$$

$$(\dot{K}/K)^* = I(0, r^*; \bar{v}) \tag{6.18}$$

$$(w/p)^* = f'(\bar{v}) \tag{6.19}$$

$$\pi^* = p^* \tag{6.20}$$

$$L(0, r^*; \bar{v}, \mu) = m^* \tag{6.21}$$

$$M = p^* K m^*. \tag{6.22}$$

$$M/K = \rho e^{\mu t}. \tag{6.8}$$

Since there is no "outside" money, there is a "dichotomy" (Patinkin, 1965, pp. 297–8) in the determination of the monetary and the non-monetary values. The complex of interest rates equates planned saving and investment at normal capacity in (6.17). Together they imply the equilibrium rate of growth in (6.18). The real wage $(w/p)^*$ of an efficiency unit of labor equals its marginal product at normal capacity in (6.19). The determination of the equilibrium level of prices is in accordance with the quantity theory of money. The supply of real balances $m^*$ equals the demand for them at the equilibrium level of interest rates in (6.21). This fixes the income velocity of circulation at $f(\bar{v})/m^*$. Then $p^*$, $w^*$, and $\pi^*$ are determined by the ratio of $M$ to $K$ via equation (6.22) along with (6.19) and (6.20), and as $M/K$ in (6.8) changes at the percentage rate $\mu$ it causes the equilibrium level of prices to do so too.

*Propagation and Impulses*

Phillips's theory, and I think Hawtrey's too, is for cycles in response to shocks. It would be possible to introduce a non-linear element via the investment function, which, in conjunction with instability of equilibrium, could produce a limit cycle in this monetarist setting just as it does in the extreme Keynesian theory of Kaldor (1940), which is dealt with in Part III.

But it is much more difficult to justify the non-linear investment function in the present situation, where $v$ is a parameter, than in the situation where there is a unique natural rate of growth to serve as a benchmark for long-term expectations. We shall not, therefore, pursue this line of thought. Instead we adopt the following

*Assumption (6.3)*

The equilibrium is asymptotically stable.

Although the propagation mechanism in this kind of model is monetary, it is not necessary that the disturbances should arise on the side of aggregate demand, through changes in $\rho$ or $\mu$ or the state of long-term expectations, for example. Shocks on the supply side can be accommodated through changes in $\bar{v}$. Examples are abrupt changes in the efficiency of labor and losses of real capital from natural causes.

*Stability Conditions*

The matrix of coefficients for the linear approximation around the equilibrium is

$$C = \begin{bmatrix} \bar{v}aH'(0)Q_x^* - bF'(1) & \bar{v}aH'(0)Q_m^* \\ -m^*[cH'(0)Q_x^* + gF'(1)/\bar{v}] & -m^*cH'(0)Q_m^* \end{bmatrix}, (6.23)$$

with

$$\text{tr } C = [\bar{v}aH'0)Q_x^* - bF'(1)] - m^*cH'(0)Q_m^* \qquad (6.24)$$

$$\det C = (ag + bc)m^*H'(0)F'(1)Q_m^* > 0. \qquad (6.25)$$

Since det $C$ is positive, Assumption (6.3) is provided for if tr $C$ is negative.

The second term in the trace is negative. When real balances are below (above) $m^*$ short-term normal prices are above (below) $p^*$.

This puts upward (downward) pressure on interest rates, tending to reduce (increase) net windfall profits and thereby to draw prices back towards their equilibrium.

But this effect of tight and easy money on net windfalls is the only unambiguously stabilizing factor. In the first (square-bracketed) term $Q_x^*$ may be positive, and sufficiently so as to outweigh the stabilizing effect of changes in $x$ on efficiency wages; for there may not be much wage flexibility when unemployment equals unfilled vacancies. There is also to be considered a "Keynesian" variant of the model, in which $b$ is zero because of full cost push. In short, values of $x$ greater or less than $\bar{v}$ may set in motion cumulative forces drawing it still farther from the equilibrium. At the point of equilibrium $\partial \dot{x}/\partial x$ may be positive.

Assumption (6.3) is therefore that $Q_m^*$ must be large enough to overcome any destabilizing effects of $x$ on $\dot{x}$.

### Damped Oscillations

The essential requirement for an endogenous theory of cycles is that the propagation mechanism should cause the economy to overshoot its equilibrium. Since the existence of oscillatory solutions, though not strictly necessary for overshooting, is the best guarantee of it, the usual approach to the theory of damped cycles is to find sufficient conditions for damped oscillations in some neighborhood of the equilibrium, that is, conditions under which the discriminant of the coefficient matrix is negative when the trace is negative.

There will be damped oscillations in some neighborhood of the equilibrium with cumulative upswings and downswings (that is, with $\partial \dot{x}/\partial x$ positive in the linear approximation) if $Q_x^*$ is sufficiently positive.

### Proof

1  There is a positive value of $Q_x^*$ at which tr $\mathbf{C}=0$ and the discriminant $D(\mathbf{C})=(\text{tr } \mathbf{C})^2 - 4 \det \mathbf{C}$ is negative.
2  At this value of $Q_x^*$ the square-bracketed term in (6.24), which is the value of $\partial \dot{x}/\partial x$ at the equilibrium, is positive and the eigenvalues of $\mathbf{C}$ are purely imaginary, so that there are oscillations with cumulative upswings and downswings.
3  But the square-bracketed term will remain positive and $D(\mathbf{C})$ will

remain negative if $Q_x^*$ is reduced somewhat below this level to a point at which tr $\mathbf{C}$, which is an increasing function of $Q_x^*$, has become negative. At this point the eigenvalues are complex conjugates with a negative real part.

Observe, however, that the mere presence of cumulative forces does not guarantee oscillations. As $Q_x^*$ is further reduced $D(\mathbf{C})$ may become positive before the square-bracketed term changes sign.

The reason for damped oscillations with cumulative movements of the employment percentage is that, when $x$ and $m$ are both decreasing (increasing), the tightening (easing) of money, though sufficient for stability, does not occur in time to prevent $x$ from overshooting its equilibrium.

We come now to an interesting point concerning the cyclical effects of wage flexibility. When $b$ is positive high enough wage flexibility (large enough $F'$) must, *cet. par.*, ensure stability (by causing tr $\mathbf{C}$ to be negative. Moreover it must prevent the occurrence of oscillations. For since $D(\mathbf{C})$ is quadratic in $F'(1)$, it increases beyond all bounds as $F'(1)$ does so. But when, in the Keynesian variant of the theory, $b$ is zero, increased wage flexibility must, *cet. par.*, induce oscillations eventually, and indeed ever more frequent oscillations as wage flexibility increases, without affecting the degree of damping. For as $F'(1)$ increases tr $\mathbf{C}$ is unchanged, but $D(\mathbf{C})$ is reduced because det $\mathbf{C}$ is increased. The imaginary part of the eigenvalues increases beyond all bounds as $F'(1)$ does so, while their real part remains constant.

Thus in the Keynesian variant damped oscillations can occur even if there is no cyclical contribution from $Q_x^*$. If $Q_x^*$ is negative there are no cumulative forces. But high flexibility of wages, and therefore of prices also via cost push, by inducing rapid tightening (easing) of money when the employment percentage is falling (rising), can cause the latter to fall below (rise above) its equilibrium. This is the special case of our model in which the cycles are like those of Phillips's theory.

*Phase Diagrams*

The elements required for a phase portrait of the trajectories are obtained in the usual way. First, in the positive quadrant of the $(x, m)$-plane draw the loci along which $\dot{x}=0$ and $\dot{m}=0$ in

(6.13) and (6.14), namely $aH[Q^*(x, m, \mu)] - bf(x/\bar{v}) = 0$ and $cH[Q^*(x, m, \mu)] + gF(x/\bar{v}) = 0$ respectively, intersecting at $(\bar{v}, m^*)$. We assume that they each define $m$ as an implicit function of $x$ for all meaningful values of the latter. We also assume, for the reason already given, that $\tau$ is less than unity. Then the gradients of these functions are

$$\frac{dm}{dx} \Big|_{\dot{x}=0} = -Q_x^*/Q_m^* + bF'(x/\bar{v})/a\bar{v}H'(Q^*)Q_m^* \qquad (6.23)$$

$$\frac{dm}{dx} \Big|_{\dot{m}=0} = -Q_x^*/Q_m^* - gF'(x/\bar{v})/c\bar{v}H'(Q^*)Q_m^*. \qquad (6.24)$$

Since by (3.43) $b/a = (1-\sigma)/(1-\tau)$ and $g/c = \omega$, we have

$$\frac{dm}{dx} \Big|_{\dot{x}=0} - \frac{dm}{dx} \Big|_{\dot{m}=0} = \frac{(1-\sigma\tau)F'(x/\bar{v})}{(1-\tau)\bar{v}H'(Q^*)Q_m^*} > 0. \qquad (6.25)$$

For all $x$ the $(\dot{x}=0)$-locus slopes upwards more steeply, or slopes downwards less steeply, than the $(\dot{m}=0)$-locus.

Secondly, insert arrows indicating the direction of the trajectories at each point. They are moving eastwards above the $(\dot{x}=0)$-locus and westwards below it; southwards above the $(\dot{m}=0)$-locus and northwards below it. For since $Q_m^*$ is positive, $\partial(\dot{x}/x)\partial m$ in (6.13) is positive and $\partial(\dot{m}/m)\partial m$ in (6.14) is negative.

The phases from which overshooting can occur are those in which the trajectories are moving northeastwards and southwestwards, that is, the phases in which $x$ and $m$ are moving in the same direction.

For the purpose of examining the behavior of the trajectories near the equilibrium point attention may be confined to the three cases illustrated below, in which both loci are monotonic functions. They are where both loci slope upwards (figure 6.1), where both loci slope downwards (figure 6.2), and where the $(\dot{x}=0)$-locus slopes upwards and the $(\dot{m}=0)$-locus slopes downwards (figure 6.3).

It is obvious from the directional arrows in figure 6.1 that if both loci slope upwards there are no oscillations. Moreover a necessary condition for oscillatory solutions is that

$$\frac{dm}{dx} \Big|_{\dot{m}=0} < 0. \qquad (6.26)$$

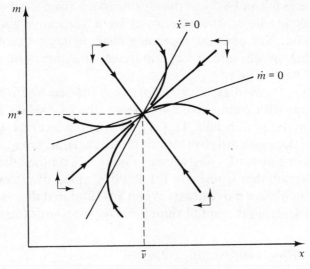

**Figure 6.1**

For even if it were zero the directional arrows would exclude oscillations. Indeed, if the ($\dot{m}=0$)-locus were horizontal there would be trajectories tending due eastwards and due westwards to the equilibrium along it.[2]

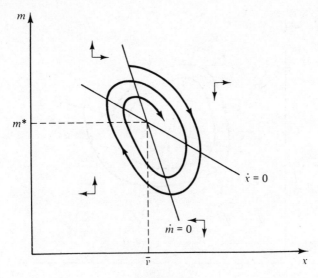

**Figure 6.2**

In figures 6.2 and 6.3 it is impossible to tell from the directional arrows alone whether the trajectories are spirals converging on the equilibrium. Nor does the foregoing analysis imply that they are converging spirals. But it has stipulated conditions under which they will be.

Figure 6.2 is the diagram appropriate to the case where there are oscillations with cumulative movements, the case where $\partial \dot{x}/\partial x$ is positive at the equilibrium. This is shown by the fact that when $x$ is displaced due eastwards (westwards) from the equilibrium it moves still farther eastwards (westwards). Figure 6.3, on the other hand, is the diagram that is relevant for Phillips's kind of cycles. There are no cumulative movements. When $x$ is displaced due eastwards (westwards) from the equilibrium it moves westwards (eastwards).

## A Comparison with Phillips's Theory

The elements from which Phillips's model is composed are as follows.

1   The ratio of normal-capacity output to the stock of capital is constant (Phillips, 1961, p. 361).

2   The economy is always in a short-period equilibrium whose equations are

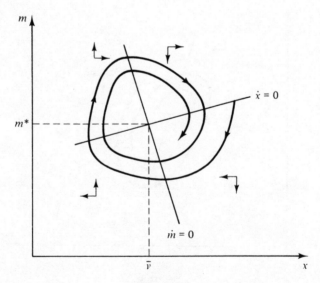

**Figure 6.3**

$$\dot{K}/K = I = S(x) \tag{6.27}$$

$$r = r(x, m,) \tag{6.28}$$

(with $r_x > 0$ and $r_m < 0$), corresponding to his equations (6) and (23).

3   The lag that has been eliminated by the postulate of perpetual short-period equilibrium is replaced (as in Kalecki, 1937) by the assumptions that $I$ has been determined by decisions taken in the past, and that its rate of increase is proportional to the excess of justified investment per unit of capital over actual investment per unit of capital. But justified investment per unit of capital $J(x, r)$ is a decreasing function of real interest rates. Therefore instead of (5.22) above we have

$$\dot{I} = \epsilon[J(x, r) - I] \tag{6.29}$$

with $J_r < 0$. This agrees with Phillips's equation (12) when his $N = 1$.

4   The proportional rate of change of money wages per worker is $W(x/\bar{v}) + \delta$, where $\delta$ is the expected inflation of money wages per worker and $W$ has the same properties as our $F$.

5   The proportional rate of change of the price level is at all times equal to the proportional rate of change of efficiency wages in terms of money. If, as Phillips supposes for simplicity, "the labor force and the normal hours worked are constant" (1961, p. 364), the growth of efficiency per worker must be $I$ when $v = \bar{v}$. Hence

$$\dot{p}/p = \dot{w}/w = W(x/\bar{v}) + \delta - I, \tag{6.30}$$

in agreement with Phillips's equation (21).

6   The nominal money-supply grows at a constant rate (p. 366):

$$\dot{M}/M = \nu = \text{constant.} \tag{6.31}$$

7   The expected inflation of money wages per worker equals $\dot{M}/M$:

$$\delta = \nu. \tag{6.32}$$

Phillips does not actually assume this, but he is willing to allow it (p. 366).

From these materials we obtain a second-order autonomous system in $x$ and $m$. Let us write

$$Z(x, m) = J[x, r(x, m)] - S(x) \tag{6.33}$$

and

$$\psi(x) = \epsilon / S'(x). \tag{6.34}$$

Then it is easily seen that the system is

$$\dot{x} = \psi(x) Z(x, m) \tag{6.35}$$

$$\dot{m} = -mW(x/\bar{v}). \tag{6.36}$$

Equation (6.35) is obtained by differentiating (6.27) with respect to time, solving for $\dot{x}$, and substituting from (6.28), (6.29), (6.33), and (6.34). Equation (6.36) follows from the definition of $m$ as $M/pK$ in (6.7) and from equations (6.27), (6.30), (6.31), and (6.32).[3]

A casual inspection of this system reveals two things. The first is that equation (6.35) has the same structure as our (6.13) has when $b=0$. This is because there is no direct effect of money-wage flexibility on employment when the economy is always in a Keynesian short-period equilibrium. The second is that $\dot{m}/m$ in (6.36) differs from $\dot{m}/m$ in our (6.14) in an important respect, namely that it does not depend on $m$. The reason for this is item 5 in the list of particulars, which implies that there is a constant markup of prices on efficiency wages. The real efficiency wage is a constant, not a function of $x$. That is why the inflation of prices does not depend on the function $Z(x, m)$, and why the model as it stands does not permit cumulative upswings and downswings.

For the consequence is that movements of real interest rates contribute to stability only by affecting $\dot{x}$. They have no direct effect on $\dot{m}$. In the matrix for the linear approximation around the equilibrium

$$\mathbf{D} = \begin{bmatrix} \psi Z_x & \psi Z_m \\ -m^*W'(1)/\bar{v} & 0 \end{bmatrix} \tag{6.37}$$

we have

$$\operatorname{tr} \mathbf{D} = \psi Z_x \tag{6.38}$$

$$\det \mathbf{D} = \psi m^* W'(1) Z_m / \bar{v} > 0, \tag{6.39}$$

so that the equilibrium is asymptotically stable if $Z_x = J_x - S'(x) + J_r r_x$ is negative, and is unstable if it is positive. Hence the stability condition precludes cumulative upswings and downswings. But there will be oscillations if $W'(1)Z_m = W'(1)J_r r_m$ is sufficiently large.

If however, the extreme assumption of cost-determined prices were dropped, it would not be difficult to extend the model so as to bring cumulative upswings and downswings into its ambit. Under perfect competition, for example, (3.36) implies that

$$\dot{p}/p = [1/x\phi(x)]\dot{x} + \dot{w}/w. \tag{6.40}$$

Substitution from (6.30) for $\dot{w}/w$ and from (6.35) for $\dot{x}$ yields

$$\dot{p}/p = \chi(x)Z(x, m) + W(x/\bar{v}) + \delta - I, \tag{6.41}$$

where

$$\chi(x) = \psi(x)/x\phi(x). \tag{6.42}$$

The revised system is therefore

$$\dot{x} = \psi(x)Z(x, m) \tag{6.35}$$

$$\dot{m} = -m[\chi(x)Z(x, m) + W(x/\bar{v})]. \tag{6.43}$$

Equation (6.43) is implied by the definition of $m$ and equations (6.27), (6.31), (6.32), and (6.41).

The structure of this system is the same as the structure of our (6.13) and (6.14) when $b=0$. Since $Z_m$ is positive and $-Z_m$ now appears in the trace, its equilibrium can be stable even if $Z_x$ is positive, so that cumulative upswings and downswings are no longer excluded.

## 6.3 Adaptive Expectations of Inflation

Cumulative movements of the employment rate are certainly an important feature of Hawtrey's cycles (Hawtrey, 1944, p. 344): "credit is *inherently unstable.* We have already referred to the 'vicious circle' of expansion and contraction. Activity causes credit expansion, credit expansion increases demand, demand invokes greater activity. Depression damps down borrowing, diminished borrowing brings with it curtailed demand, curtailed demand means more depression." Less certain, however, is the mechanism whereby tight and easy money operates to reverse them. Is it through the effect of high and low prices on the supply of real balances? On the one hand he says: "That the transition from activity to depression was marked by a restriction of credit occasioned by a shortage of cash reserves in the banks is a fact proved by experience'' (p. 342). This could be construed in the following way. In our temporary-equilibrium equation (3.2) $\alpha$ is positive and the law of reflux (which Hawtrey seems not to have rejected) determines the quantity of deposits. When high prices cause $m$ to fall below $L^*$ they create a shortage of reserves, active hoarding by the commercial banks, high interest rates, and net windfall losses.

Why should the instability of credit not have been removed by the imposition of Say's Law? Because credit policy was geared to the international gold standard (Hawtrey, 1944, pp. 341–9):

We have now shown that the variations of effective demand, which are the real substance of the trade cycle, must be traced to movements in bank credit. But we have still to explain why and how such movements in bank credit will occur. Under pre-war conditions the creation of bank credit was governed by the supply of gold. (p. 341).

I started by saying that since the war there has been no trade cycle. This is in itself a valuable confirmation of the monetary explanation. For if the cause of the trade cycle is to be found in the gradual progress of a credit expansion in an international gold standard system, we should expect that when there is no such system there would be no cycle. (p. 348).

The too ready acceptance of reserve proportions as the guide to credit policy was the real cause of the trade cycle before the war. (p. 349).

On the other hand there are passages suggesting that high and low prices are not enough to turn things around. Monetary policy must respond actively to the upswings and downswings:

The trade cycle is composed of periods of good trade, characterised by rising prices and low unemployment percentages, alternating with periods of bad trade, characterised by falling prices and high unemployment percentages. (p. 331)

. . . credit is *inherently unstable* . . . a small or casual credit movement, whether expansion or contraction, tends to exaggerate itself. Once started, it grows, and will continue growing till the banks take active steps to stop it. (p. 344)

A complication is introduced into the control of credit in that the psychology of the trader influences the velocity of circulation of money. When prices are expected to rise, people hasten to spend money, and hold smaller balances relatively to the extent of their transactions; when prices are expected to fall, they lose little by letting balances accumulate. The result is that a contraction of credit may have very little visible effect upon the amount of bank deposits. Borrowing is checked, but because balances are less quickly spent, existing indebtedness is not paid off. In 1920 when bank rate in London was raised to 7 per cent, and the most intense deflation was set on foot, the total amount of bank deposits in England actually increased. (p. 348)[4]

Inflations and deflations create expectations of their continuance, thereby affecting the demand for deposits and the supply of credit (loanable funds). It seems, therefore, that Hawtrey's ideas would be more accurately conveyed in a model for cycles of inflation and employment, in which monetary policy must cope with the fact that inflation will "create its own draught" (Wicksell, 1936, p. 96). Adaptive expectations of inflation would destabilize the equilibrium unless the central bank pursued an appropriately active monetary policy. For suppose that Assumption (6.1) is replaced by the following

### Assumption (6.1)'

The expected inflation of short-term normal prices $\lambda$ is adaptive. Its motion is governed by the function

$$\dot{\lambda} = \zeta(\dot{p}/p - \lambda), \tag{6.44}$$

which is sign-preserving and strictly increasing.

If monetary policy continues to be in accordance with Assumption (6.2), the dynamic behavior of the economy will be described by the following third-order autonomous system, obtained from (6.1), (6.2), (6.11), and (6.44):

$$\dot{x} = x\{aH[Q^*(x, m, \lambda)] - bF(x/\bar{v})\} \tag{6.45}$$

$$\dot{m} = m\{\mu - \lambda - cH[Q^*(x, m, \lambda) - gF(x/\bar{v})\}. \tag{6.46}$$

$$\dot{\lambda} = \zeta\{cH[Q^*(x, m, \lambda)] + gF(x/\bar{v})\}. \tag{6.47}$$

The equilibrium $(x^*, m^*, \lambda^*)$ is the same as that of (6.13) and (6.14), but the conditions for asymptotic stability are more arduous.

The matrix for the linear approximation.

$$
E=\begin{bmatrix}
\bar{v}aH'(0)Q_x^* - bF'(1) \\
-m^*[cH'(0)Q_x^* + gF'(1)/\bar{v}] \\
\zeta'(0)[cH'(0)Q_x^* + gF'(1)/\bar{v}] \\
\bar{v}aH'(0)Q_m^* \qquad\qquad \bar{v}aH'(0)Q_\lambda^* \\
-m^*cH'(0)Q_m^* \quad -m^*[1+cH'(0)Q_\lambda^*] \\
\zeta'(0)cH'0)Q_m^* \qquad\qquad \zeta'(0)cH'(0)Q_\lambda^*
\end{bmatrix}, \qquad (6.48)
$$

has

$$
\operatorname{tr} E = [\bar{v}aH'(0)Q_x^* - bF'(1)] - cH'(0)[m^*Q_m^* - \zeta'(0)Q_l^*] \tag{6.49}
$$

$$
\Sigma E = (ag+bc)H'(0)F'(1)[m^*Q_m^* - \zeta'(0)Q_\lambda^*] \\
+ m^*cH'(0)\zeta'(0)Q_m^*, \tag{6.50}
$$

$$
\det E = -(ag+bc)m^*H'(0)\zeta'(0)F'(1)Q_m^* < 0 \tag{6.51}
$$

where $\Sigma E$ is the sum of the second-order principal minors. The determinant is negative, but in the trace the stabilizing influence of high and low prices via $-m^*Q_m^*$ is weakened, if not overcome, by the destabilizing influence of high and low expectations of inflation via $\zeta'(0)Q_\lambda^*$. For this term must be positive if $L_\lambda$ is negative. Thus even if $m^*Q_m^* - \zeta'(0)Q_\lambda^*$ is positive it may not be large enough to prevent $\operatorname{tr} E > 0$. Moreover even if the trace is negative the third Routh-Hurwitz condition

$$
\det E > (\operatorname{tr} E)(\Sigma E) \tag{6.52}
$$

may be violated.

Since, from equations (3.7) and (3.8),

$$
m^*Q_m^* - \zeta'(0)Q_\lambda^* = -[\gamma(I_r - S_r)(m^* + \zeta'(0)L_\lambda)]/\Delta, \tag{6.53}
$$

the condition that this term should be positive is that $-\zeta'(0)L_\lambda/m^* < 1$. This is the same as the stability condition $\alpha\beta < 1$ given by Cagan in his study of hyperinflations (Cagan, 1956, section V, pp. 64–5). Our $-L_\lambda/m^*$ is Cagan's $\alpha$ and our $\zeta'(0)$ is his $\beta$.

Cagan himself could conclude that this condition is sufficient for stability. But that is because, since he was not concerned with cyclical movements, he was content to assume perpetual full employment. Naturally enough the same result is obtained from our system under this assumption.

A straightforward route to perpetual clearing of the labor

market is by way of the assumptions that (1) money wages are perfectly flexible, in the sense that $F$ is infinitely positive (negative) when $x/\bar{v}$ is greater than (less than) unity; and (2) there is no cost push. Then at the outset of each instant

$$w=pf'(\bar{v}) \tag{6.54}$$

$$x=\bar{v}, \tag{6.55}$$

and from one instant to the next

$$\dot{p}/p=\lambda+H(Q^*), \tag{6.56}$$

from (3.29) with $\sigma=0$.

In these circumstances the third-order dynamic system above reduces to one of the second-order in $m$ and $\lambda$:

$$\dot{m}=m\{\mu-\lambda-H[Q^*(\bar{v}, m, \lambda)]\} \tag{6.57}$$

$$\dot{\lambda}=\varsigma\{H[Q^*(\bar{v}, m, \lambda)]\} \tag{6.58}$$

The coefficient matrix for the linear approximation around the equilibrium of this system is the submatrix obtained by deleting the first row and column of $E$ and putting $c=1$. Let us call it $E_{11}$. Since

$$\operatorname{tr} E_{11} = -H'(0)[m^*Q_m^* - \varsigma'(0)Q_\lambda^*] \tag{6.59}$$

$$\det E_{11} = m^*H'(0)\varsigma'(0)Q_m^* > 0, \tag{6.60}$$

the equilibrium is asymptotically stable provided that the "Cagan condition" above is satisfied.[5]

But the message conveyed by Cagan's analysis in his section VI (1956) is more optimistic than this. It is that under full employment, at least, the stability of equilibrium does not even require the "Cagan condition" (p. 75). If that were indeed the case one might be tempted to conclude that the stability problem posed by adaptive expectations may not be very serious even in the context of business cycles.

It is important, therefore, to note that the source of the message is a rather odd assumption. Essentially it is that the dynamics of $p$ are governed, not by (6.56), but by an equation which in our system would take the form

$$\dot{p}/p=\mu+H(Q^*). \tag{6.61}$$

Together with (6.10) and (6.44) this implies that the system

$$\dot{m}/m = -H[Q^*(\bar{v}, m, \lambda)] \tag{6.62}$$

$$\dot{\lambda} = \zeta\{\mu - \lambda + H[Q^*(\bar{v}, m, \lambda)]\} \tag{6.63}$$

should replace (6.57) and (6.58).[6] It is autonomous in $m$ and $\lambda$ if $\mu$ is a constant. The coefficient matrix for the linear approximation is

$$\mathbf{F} = \begin{bmatrix} -m^*H'(0)Q_m^* & -m^*H'(0)Q_\lambda^* \\ \zeta'(0)H'(0)Q_m^* & \zeta'(0)H'(0)Q_\lambda^* - \zeta'(0) \end{bmatrix}, \tag{6.64}$$

with

$$\text{tr } \mathbf{F} = -H'(0)[m^*Q_m^* - \zeta'(0)Q_\lambda^*] - \zeta'(0) \tag{6.65}$$

$$\det \mathbf{F} = m^*H'(0)\zeta'(0)Q_m^* > 0. \tag{6.66}$$

Thus the trace can be negative even if the "Cagan condition", that the square-bracketed term should be positive, is violated.

The reason for the lighter stability condition in this model is that, since a change in $\lambda$ does not affect $\dot{p}/p$ directly, it has a tendency to reduce the size of the gap between them, and therefore to reduce the absolute magnitude of $\dot{\lambda}$.

But it is paradoxical, to say the least, that the course of real balances should be entirely independent of the course of the nominal money-supply, and that, when an equilibrium is disturbed by a change in $\mu$, actual inflation should immediately change so as to equal the new $\mu$ even if expected inflation remained initially equal to the old $\mu$.

### 6.4 Cycles of Inflation and Employment

The upshot of the matter is that if inflation does create its own draught a theory of damped monetary cycles under adaptive expectations of inflation should assume that the central bank secures the stability of equilibrium by an active monetary policy. It seems reasonable to suppose that the monetary authority shares the general expectation of inflation. In that case we may replace Assumption (6.2) by

Assumption (6.2)'. At the outset of each instant the central bank chooses the potential nominal supply of deposits in such a way as to make the supply of real balances a decreasing function of the expected rate of inflation. Its policy is expressed by the function

$$m = m(\lambda; \theta), \tag{6.67}$$

where $m_\lambda$ is negative and $\theta$ is a shift parameter with $m_\theta$ positive.

## The Dynamic System

From (6.1), (6.2), (6.44), and (6.67) we obtain the following second-order autonomous system in $x$ and $\lambda$:

$$\dot{x} = x\{aH[Q^*(x, m, \lambda)] - bF(x/\bar{v})\} \tag{6.68}$$

$$\dot{\lambda} = \zeta\{cH[Q^*(x, m, \lambda)] + gF(x/\bar{v})\} \tag{6.69}$$

$$m = m(\lambda; \theta). \tag{6.67}$$

Thus under Assumptions (6.1)' and (6.2)', given respectively by (6.44) and (6.67), the monetary factor affects the temporary equilibrium not through the level of short-term normal prices but through their expected rate of change.

## Equilibrium and Stability

The equilibrium of the non-monetary quantities is still given by equations (6.15) through (6.19). But the monetary equilibrium is now

$$\pi^* = p \tag{6.70}$$

$$L(0, r^*; \bar{v}, \lambda^*) = m(\lambda^*; \theta) \tag{6.71}$$

$$(\dot{p}/p)^* = \lambda^*. \tag{6.72}$$

For any given value of the parameter $\theta$ the equilibrium rate of inflation of prices and efficiency wages is unique, but since the central bank has chosen $M/pK$, not $M/K$, the price levels themselves depend on the historical record. The equilibrium does not determine them. Notice that a change in $\theta$ changes $\lambda^*$ in the same direction, but has no effect on the other equilibrium values.

For a theory of damped cycles it is necessary to retain Assumption (6.3), that the equilibrium is asymptotically stable. But since the matrix of coefficents for the linear approximation around the equilibrium

$$\mathbf{G} = \begin{bmatrix} \bar{v}aH'(0)Q_x^* - bF'(1) & \bar{v}aH'(0)(Q_m^*m_\lambda + Q_\lambda^*) \\ \zeta'0)[cH'(0)Q_x^* + gF'(1)/\bar{v}] & \zeta'(0)cH'(0)(Q_m^*m_\lambda + Q_x^*) \end{bmatrix} \tag{6.73}$$

has

$$\text{tr}\,\mathbf{G} = [\bar{v}aH'(0)Q_x^* - bF'(1)]$$
$$+ \zeta'(0)cH'(0)(Q_m^*m_\lambda + Q_\lambda^*) \tag{6.74}$$

$$\det\mathbf{G} = -(ag+bc)\zeta'(0)H'(0)F'(1)(Q_m^*m_\lambda + Q_\lambda^*), \tag{6.75}$$

the stabilization problem posed by Assumptions (6.1)′ and (6.2)′ is clearly not a trivial one.

In the first place the term $Q_x^*m_\lambda + Q_\lambda^*$ must be negative if the determinant is to be positive. If the term is positive the equilibrium is a saddle point. Thus there is a stabilization problem even in the special case of full wage indexation ($\tau=0$) in which $x$ approaches $\bar{v}$ monotonically because $a=0$ in equation (6.68). The eigenvalues are $-bF'(1)$ and $\zeta'(0)cH'(0)(Q_m^*m_\lambda + Q_\lambda^*)$, and if $Q_m^*m_\lambda + Q_\lambda^*$ is positive $\lambda$ will increase or decrease forever unless it is initially on the stable branch.

In the second place the term $\zeta'(0)cH'(0)(Q_m^*m_\lambda + Q_\lambda^*)$ in the trace must be sufficiently negative to overcome the cumulative forces that are present if the square-bracketed term is positive.

$Q_m^*m_\lambda + Q_\lambda^*$ is the partial derivative of $Q^*[x, m(\lambda; \theta), \lambda]$ with respect to $\lambda$. From (3.7) and (3.8) we have

$$Q_m^*m_\lambda + Q_\lambda^* = -[\gamma(I_r - S_r)(m_\lambda - L_\lambda)]/\Delta. \tag{6.76}$$

Therefore to provide for stability $m_\lambda$ must not only be less than (more negative than) $L_\lambda$ but sufficently so as to make tr G negative.

From (3.10) and (3.11) the partial derivative of $r^*[x, m(\lambda; \theta), \lambda]$ with respect to $\lambda$ is

$$r_m^*m_\lambda + r_\lambda^* = [\gamma(I_Q - S_Q - 1)(m_\lambda - L_\lambda)]/\Delta. \tag{6.77}$$

This means that the stabilizing tendency of high and low real interest rates, which in the previous case was brought about by high and low prices respectively, must here be brought about by the central bank's active countermeasures against the destabilizing influence of high and low expected rates of inflation. "Leaning against the wind" is not enough. Rather, the direction of the wind must be reversed.

There is, however, one potentially mitigating circumstance. If $Q_m^*m_\lambda + Q_\lambda^*$ is negative its stabilizing influence is greater the larger is $\zeta'(0)$. When the wind is favorable its very strength becomes advantageous.

## Damped Oscillations

In view of its formal resemblance to the system consisting of (6.13) and (6.14) we shall not be surprised to find that this, too, is a model which can produce both Hawtrey's cycles with cumulative forces and Phillips's cycles without them. Comparing (6.24) and (6.25) with (6.74) and (6.75) we see that tr $\mathbf{C}$ and det $\mathbf{C}$ differ from tr $\mathbf{G}$ and det $\mathbf{G}$ only in that the term $-Q_m^*$ in tr $\mathbf{C}$ and det $\mathbf{C}$ is replaced by the term $\zeta'(0)(Q_m^* m_\lambda + Q_x^*)$ in tr $\mathbf{G}$ and det $\mathbf{G}$. Therefore if the stability conditions are satisfied (1) there will be damped oscillations with cumulative upswings and downswings if $Q_x^*$ is sufficiently positive; and (2) there will be damped oscillations without them if, though $Q_x^*$ is negative, full cost push is combined with sufficiently high flexibility of efficiency wages.

In case (1), when $x$ is decreasing (increasing) and $\lambda$ is increasing (decreasing), the tightening (easing) of money due to the central bank's response to expected inflation does not occur in time to prevent the employment percentage from overshooting its equilibrium. In case (2) overshooting occurs because high flexibility of efficiency wages, and therefore of short-term normal prices via cost push, induces rapid revisions of inflationary expectations and hence rapid tightening (easing) of money when the employment percentage is falling (rising).

## Phase Diagrams

Since the sign of $\lambda$ is unrestricted, the phase portraits occupy the right half of the $(x, \lambda)$-plane. From (6.67), (6.68) and (6.69) we find that the loci along which $\dot{x}=0$ on the one hand and $\dot{\lambda}=0$ on the other hand are given respectively by the equations $aH\{Q^*[x, m(\lambda; \theta), \lambda]\} - bF(x/\bar{v})=0$ and $cH\{Q^*[x, m(\lambda; \theta), \lambda]\} + gF(x/\bar{v})=0$, intersecting at $(\bar{v}, \lambda^*)$. If $\tau$ is less than unity and these equations each define $\lambda$ as a function of $x$ the gradients of the two functions are

$$\frac{d\lambda}{dx}\Big|_{\dot{x}=0} = \frac{-Q_x^*/(Q_m^* m_\lambda + Q_x^*)}{+bF'(x/\bar{v})/a\bar{v}H'(Q^*)(Q_m^* m_\lambda + Q_x^*)} \qquad (6.78)$$

$$\frac{d\lambda}{dx}\Big|_{\dot{\lambda}=0} = \frac{-Q_x^*/(Q_m^* m_\lambda + Q_x^*)}{-gF'(x/\bar{v})/c\bar{v}H'(Q^*)(Q_m^* m_\lambda + Q_x^*)}, \qquad (6.79)$$

and

$$\frac{d\lambda}{dx}\bigg|_{\dot{x}=0} - \frac{d\lambda}{dx}\bigg|_{\dot{\lambda}=0} = \frac{(1-\sigma\tau)F'(x/\bar{v})}{(1-\tau)\bar{v}H'(Q^*)(Q_m^* m_\lambda + Q_\lambda^*)} < 0,$$

(6.80)

because stability requires that the denominator should be negative. The $(\dot{x}=0)$-locus slopes downward more steeply, or slopes upwards less steeply, than the $(\dot{\lambda}=0)$-locus.

The trajectories move westwards above the $(\dot{x}=0)$-locus and eastwards below it; southwards above the $(\dot{\lambda}=0)$-locus and northwards above it. For $\partial(\dot{x}/x)/\partial\lambda$ and $\partial\dot{\lambda}/\partial\lambda$ are both negative when $Q_m^* m_\lambda + Q_\lambda^*$ is negative.

The phases from which overshooting can occur are those in which the trajectories are moving northwestwards and southeastwards. These are the phases in which $x$ and $\lambda$ are traveling in opposite directions. When, for example, employment increases, it is encouraged to continue increasing as decreasing expected inflation leads to easier money.

When, as in figure 6.4 below, both loci slope downwards the directional arrows preclude oscillations. But the trajectories may

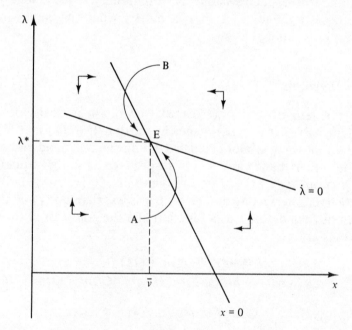

**Figure 6.4**

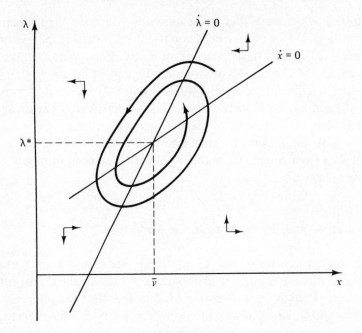

**Figure 6.5**

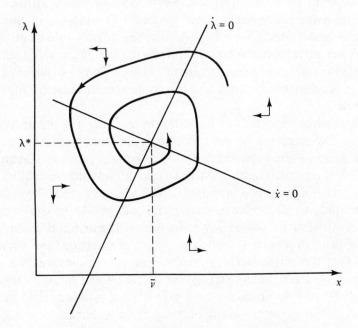

**Figure 6.6**

be spirals when both loci slope upwards (figure 6.5) or when the $(\dot{x}=0)$-locus slopes downwards and the $(\dot{\lambda}=0)$-locus slopes upwards (figure 6.6). The phase portrait of oscillations with cumulative movements of the employment percentage must be drawn in figure 6.5, where a displacement of $x$ due eastwards (westwards) from the equilibrium causes it to move still farther eastwards (westwards). Finally the phase protrait of oscillations without cumulative movements must be drawn in figure 6.6, where displacements of $x$ due eastwards (westwards) from the equilibrium cause it to move westwards (eastwards).

### 6.5 Inflation and Unemployment: the Trade-off

In a closed economy, or in an open economy with variable exchange rates, if commercial banks are subject to the law of reflux and there is passive net hoarding of deposits these monetary cycles can be eliminated simply by invoking Say's law. Even so there may be objections to maintaining such a policy. An insuperable objection would be full cost push. For as we observed above (ch. 4, section 4.6) full cost push and Say's law are incompatible. But putting aside this extreme case we can still conceive of circumstances under which a steady regime of Say's law would be distasteful. They arise from the fact that, while the law ensures that neither inflation nor the unemployment rate will be influenced by aggregate demand, it does nothing to determine their equilibrium values.

Thus when expectations of inflation are adaptive the monetary policy characterized by Assumption (6.2)′ may appear attractive from time to time, particularly if the central bank has acquired sufficient control over the system to rule out not only instability but also overshooting. For suppose, on the one hand, that the government, judging the average unemployment rate to be too high, is willing to secure a temporary reduction of the unemployment rate at the price of a permanently higher rate of inflation; and suppose also that the phase portrait of the system is in accordance with figure 6.4. Then the desired course of events will be set in train if the central bank chooses a higher level of $\theta$ provided that such a policy of easier money is the only significant shock to the system. Both the $(\dot{x}=0)$-locus and the $(\dot{\lambda}=0)$-locus will be higher than before, but they will still intersect at $\bar{v}$. For nothing has occurred to alter the equilibrium value of $x$. Initially both $x$ and $\lambda$ will rise (along the trajectory starting from the old equilibrium point A in the diagram). But the necessity to maintain stability forces tighter money as $\lambda$ rises, causing $x$ to return to its equilibrium at $\bar{v}$ without overshooting it. The new equilibrium (at point E in the diagram) will have a higher expected rate of inflation $\lambda^*$, and a higher actual rate of inflation equal to it, but the same unemployment rate. In the interval during which the unemployment rate is rising it is possible, but so far as I can see not necessary, that the "stagflation" effect (where both the unemployment rate and the rate of inflation of actual prices are simultaneously rising) may be observed.

If, on the other hand, the government is determined to fight inflation even at the cost of a temporary rise in the unemployment percentage it can do so by decreasing $\theta$. In the absence of overshooting this will bring about exactly the opposite sequence of events (illustrated by the trajectory starting at the old equilibrium point B), terminating at a lower expected and actual rate of inflation but the original equilibrium unemployment percentage. Perhaps we should call this the "Volcker" effect! Indeed, any desired reduction of inflation with minimal effects on employment could be engineered through a sequence of small decreases in $\theta$.

## Notes

1   Not quite the same, however. Since Tobin's "M-Model" has adaptive expectations of inflation, it is more accurately represented by the special case of full wage indexation in the third-order system of section 6.3.

2   When the gradient of the ($\dot{m}=0$)-locus is zero at the equilibrium we have $c\bar{v}H'(0)Q_x^* = -gF'(1)$. Substituting this into tr $\mathbf{C}$ we find that the eigenvalues are real and negative, viz. $-(ag+bc)F'(1)/c$ and $m^*cH'(0)Q_m^*$. When $Q_x^*$ is decreased below this point, so that the gradient becomes positive, $D(\mathbf{C})$ must be positive.

3   Phillips's world differs from ours in that rising labor productivity tends to reduce prices, not to increase money wages per worker. Nevertheless the difference need not affect the dynamics. For suppose that Phillips's assumption about the behavior of money wages per worker is replaced by the assumption that the rate of change of efficiency wages in terms of money is $\dot{w}/w = \lambda + F(x/\bar{v})$. This follows from our (6.3) if wage indexation is zero ($\tau=0$); for then, by (3.43), $h=0$ and $c=1$. In that case, since item 5 in the

catalogue asserts that the inflation of prices equals the inflation of efficiency wages, we shall have

$$\dot{p}/p = \lambda + F(x/\bar{v}) \tag{6.30}'$$

instead of (6.30). But under our Assumptions (6.1) and 6.2) we shall still obtain an equation like (6.36), namely

$$\dot{m}/m = -F(x/\bar{v}). \tag{6.36}'$$

Thus the dynamics are the same provided that the monetary policies assumed are appropriately different. Whereas (6.36) requires constancy of $\dot{M}/M$, (6.36)' requires constancy of $\dot{M}/M - \dot{K}/K$.

4   It is ironical that, if Hawtrey is correct, the amount of bank deposits in 1920, the year in which C. R. Phillips's *Bank Credit* was published, increased in accordance with the law of reflux.

5   For a fuller analysis of an essentially similar model with full employment and a fixed factor supply ratio see Stein (1971, ch. 5).

6   Cagan's assumption about the behavior of prices is implicit in his postulate that $\dot{m}/m$ is a function only of the excess demand for real balances (equation (20), p. 74). For if $\dot{m}/m = N(L - m)$ (where $N$ is a sign-preserving and increasing function), then $\dot{p}/p = \mu - N$. Notice that this postulate is implied by our version of his system if in (3.2) above $\alpha$ is not zero. For then $Q^* = -(\gamma/\alpha)[L^* - m]$.

# PART III

## Macrodynamics with a Variable Ratio of Available Factors

# 7

# "Keynesian" Overinvestment Cycles

---

### 7.1 The Natural Rate of Growth

Henceforward we shall be occupied with theories which arise from the assumption that the factor-supply ratio is a variable because the rates of growth of the labor force and of efficiency per unit of labor are parameters. In the equation

$$\dot{v}/v = n - I^*(x, m, \lambda) \tag{3.39}$$

$n$, the "natural" rate of growth (Harrod, 1948, p. 87), is a datum. A long-period equilibrium with $\dot{v}=0$ is either a stationary state or a state of exogenously determined steady growth – Cassel's "simplest case of a uniformly progressing economic system" (Cassel, 1932, p. 34).

### 7.2 Overinvestment

"Over-investment" is the label attached by Haberler to theories of the business cycle whose central theme is "over-development of industries which produce producers' goods or capital goods in relation to industries producing consumers' goods" (Haberler, 1963, p. 29). Strictly speaking such theories require a two-sector disaggregation of the economy. But in fact essentially similar cycles are implied without disaggregation when the central theme is stated as overaccumulation of capital. The rate of accumulation of capital ($\dot{K}/K$) is higher in the boom and lower in the slump than that which can be sustained in a long-period equilibrium ($n$). It is convenient, therefore, to use the term "over-investment" for this feature, particularly as it is the central theme in a wider group of business-cycle theories than those covered by Haberler's definition.

### 7.3 The "Keynesian" Model and its Long-period Equilibrium

For the "Keynesian" overinvestment theories the constant natural rate of growth will be combined with the extreme Keynesian assumptions of chapter 5.

*Assumption (7.1)*

Monetary policy is ineffective because neither planned investment nor planned saving depends on interest rates:

$$I_r = S_r = 0. \tag{5.3}$$

Some of our authors would rather assume that the reason why the level of interest rates does not appear in the planned investment and planned saving functions is not because it can have no effect on them but because it is itself uniquely determined by the level of activity $x$. This is the position taken, for example, by Kaldor (1960, Essay 8, p. 178, footnote 1):

$S$ and $I$ are, of course, both functions of the rate of interest in addition to the level of activity. But the rate of interest, at any rate in the first approximation, could itself be regarded as a single-valued function of the level of activity, and thus its influence incorporated in the $S(x)$ and $I(x)$ functions.

But whatever the justification of this assumption may be, it yields theories that are just like those which rely on Assumption (7.1).

*Assumption (7.2)*

Efficiency wages in term of money are inflexible:

$$F(x/v) = 0. \tag{5.4}$$

Finally, we can simplify matters without distorting the picture if we eliminate the feedback from windfall profits to planned investment and planned saving.

*Assumption (7.3)*

Windfalls have no effect on $I$ and $S$:

$$I_Q = S_Q = 0. \tag{7.1}$$

But the inflexibility of wages and the impotence of monetary policy create a problem in regard to the existence and uniqueness of a long-period equilibrium. The dynamic equations for $\dot{x}$ and $\dot{v}$ are

$$\dot{x} = xaH[Q^*(x)] \tag{7.2}$$

$$\dot{v} = v[n - I(x)] \tag{7.3}$$

when $F = 0$ and the partial derivatives of $Q^*$ and $I^*$ with respect to $m$ and $\lambda$ are zero. Therefore there is normally no solution such that $\dot{x} = \dot{v} = 0$. Except by a lucky chance there will be no $x^*$ at which the temporary-equilibrium equations

$$Q^* = I(x) - S(x) \tag{7.4}$$

$$\dot{K}/K = I(x) \tag{7.5}$$

can be satisfied with both $Q^* = 0$ and $(\dot{K}/K)^* = n$, that is, with $I(x^*) = S(x^*) = n$. And even if there were such an $x^*$ there would be nothing to determine $v^*$.

This is the difficulty referred to by Kaldor as "Mr. Harrod's problem" (Kaldor, 1960, Essay 9, p. 204), namely how to link warranted rates of growth, that is, rates of growth which are consistent with saving-investment equilibrium, with growth at the natural rate.

Actually the problem is not especially connected with growth. It arises from the fact that the levels of both planned investment $KI$ and planned saving $KS$ are positively homogeneous functions (of the first degree) of the demand for efficiency labor and the stock of capital and are not also dependent on the supply of real balances.

Let us write $KI = U(N^d, K)$ and $SI = V(N^d, K)$. In a long-period equilibrium

$$U(N^d, K) - nK = 0 \tag{7.6}$$

$$V(N^d, K) - nK = 0 \tag{7.7}$$

at each point of time. When the functions are positively homogeneous these conditions are expressed by the matrix equation

$$\begin{bmatrix} U_{N^d} & U_K - n \\ V_{N^d} & V_K - n \end{bmatrix} \begin{bmatrix} N^d \\ K \end{bmatrix} = \begin{bmatrix} 0 \\ 0 \end{bmatrix}. \tag{7.8}$$

There are therefore two possibilities: (1) that the Jacobian matrix is everywhere non-singular, in which case there is a unique "equilibrium" at $N^d = K = 0$; and (2) that the Jacobian matrix is singular for some values of the variables, in which case there may be rays of non-negative equilibria. Hence either (1) there is no economically meaningful equilibrium, or (2) there is a multiplicity of equilibria.

The resolution of this problem has been to invoke *autonomous expenditures* (see Sawyer, 1987) growing at the natural rate. Assume that, while planned investment and planned saving are positively homogeneous in their arguments, one of these arguments is the supply of labor in efficiency units $N^s$. It need not be present in both functions, but it must be present in one of them. If $N^s$ enters positively into the consumption function, and therefore negatively into the saving function, there is autonomous consumption, consumption that is not induced by current incomes or wealth; and if it enters positively into the investment function there is autonomous investment, investment that is not entirely induced by current or recent experience. The equilibrium will be a stationary state if $N^s$ is constant and a progressive state if it is growing at the rate $n$.

Autonomous consumption may be ascribed to government spending growing at the natural rate. Another reason for it was suggested by Kaldor in his 1951 review of Hicks's *Trade Cycle*. Consumption by the unemployed is at the expense of planned saving, which is therefore a decreasing function of unemployment:

It seems obvious that the proportion of income saved in a community would be lower the higher is the rate of unemployment: since the unemployed will continue to consume something, and the propensity to consume of the others (even in the absence of budgetary deficits) will not normally be decreased sufficiently to offset this. Hence while the proportion of income saved might be regarded as a given proportion of full-employment income, the average propensity might still be treated as a diminishing function of the rate of unemployment. In that case, however, the Harrod equilibrium could be attained with varying rates of growth and correspondingly higher or lower rates of unemployment. (Kaldor, 1960, Essay 9, p. 206)

See also Matthews (1955).

The rationale for autonomous investment is the idea that long-term expectations increase with $N^s$. In his *Theory of the Trade Cycle* Hicks (1950, pp. 96–7) adopted a rather extreme version of this postulate by adding to "induced investment" (that which depends on current or recent experience) a term which grows at the natural rate. Hicks assumed this term, which is proportional to $N^s$, to be growing at a positive rate in order to guarantee the economy's recovery from the slump.

There is some indication that even in his original 1939 *Essay in Dynamic Theory* Harrod's own solution was also to make investment decisions depend on $N^s$. For he says there (Harrod, 1952, Essay 13, p. 269), "Some outlays of capital have no direct relation to the current increase in output. They may be related to a prospective long-period increase of activity, and be but slightly influenced, if at all, by the current increase of trade. Or they may be induced by new inventions . . ." and introduces a formula for the warranted rate which makes it depend on the ratio of these outlays, designated by the symbol $K$, to the current level of income. This is confirmed in his supplementary essay (Harrod, 1952, Essay 14, p. 280), where he compares the outlays so designated with Hicks's autonomous investment: "Autonomous investment (my $K$) may be regarded as the investment flowing from orders that would be given whatever the current out-turn. Autonomous investment is decided upon in consequence of considerations of longer range." But his reaction to Hicks's treatment was that by simply adding a term growing at the natural rate one draws too sharp a distinction between long-period and short-period motives for investment. Long-range investment is not wholly independent of current or recent experience:

On the other hand, it is hard to think of any investment which will not be made subject to reconsideration if a depression is sufficiently prolonged and intense. . . . This was one reason for making me doubt whether Mr. Hicks can be right in attributing revival to the long-run upward slope of the autonomous investment curve, since it is in the period just prior to revival that the shift of items out of the autonomous category is likely to be greatest. (Harrod, 1952, p. 281)

In our system this solution to the homogeneity problem is implemented by making either $KI$ or $KS$ positively homogeneous in the demand for labor in efficiency units, the stock of capital and the supply of labor in efficiency units, that is, in $N^d$, $K$, and $N^s$. The consequence is that $v=N^s/K$ appears as a parameter of the temporary equilibrium and as a variable in the equations of motion. Instead of (7.4) and (7.5) we have

$$Q^* = I(x, v) - S(x, v) \qquad (7.9)$$

$$\dot{K}/K = I(x, v) \qquad (7.10)$$

with

$$I_v \geq 0 \text{ and } S_v \leq 0 \qquad (7.11)$$

and

$$I_v S_v \neq 0. \qquad (7.12)$$

and instead of the dynamic equations (7.2) and (7.3) we have

$$\dot{x} = xaH[Q^*(x, v)] \qquad (7.13)$$

$$\dot{v} = v[(n - I(x, v)]. \qquad (7.14)$$

There may then be a unique long-period equilibrium which satisfies the equations

$$I(x^*, v^*) = S(x^*, v^*) = n \qquad (7.15)$$

and at which there is "Keynesian" unemployment, in the sense that

$$x^* < v^*. \qquad (7.16)$$

The matrix of the linear approximation around such an equilibrium is

$$\mathbf{H} = \begin{bmatrix} x^*aH'(0)Q_x^* & x^*aH'(0)Q_v^* \\ -v^*I_x & -v^*I_v \end{bmatrix}. \qquad (7.17)$$

Since by (7.9) $Q_x^* = I_x - S_x$ and $Q_v^* = I_v - S_v$ we have

$$\text{tr } \mathbf{H} = x^*aH'(0)(I_x - S_x) - v^*I_v \qquad (7.18)$$

$$\det \mathbf{H} = x^*v^*aH'(0)(I_v S_x - S_v I_x). \qquad (7.19)$$

### 7.4 Kalecki's Theory of Fluctuations

*The Autonomous-consumption Model*

The damped overinvestment cycles of Kalecki (1937, 1939) and Samuelson (1939) are obtained under the assumption that, while autonomous expenditures influence aggregate demand, they have no effect on the rate of accumulation. This is the case in our model when there is autonomous consumption but no autonomous investment, so that the second-order system is

$$\dot{x} = xaH[Q^*(x, v)] \qquad\qquad (7.13)$$

$$\dot{v} = v[n - I(x)]. \qquad\qquad (7.3)$$

*Stability*

The equilibrium is assumed to satisfy (7.16). Since $I_v = 0$ it will be asymptotically stable if the marginal inducement to invest is positive but less than the marginal propensity to save, that is, if $0 < I_x(x^*) < S_x(x^*, v^*)$.

*"Slightly Damped Oscillations"*

The trajectories in a neighborhood of the equilibrium will be spirals converging to it if $I_x$ is sufficiently positive there without violating the stability condition. For since on the borderline between stability and instability where $I_x = S_x$ the discriminant is negative, it must remain negative if $I_x$ is slightly less than $S_x$.

Apparently it was Kalecki who originated the idea, later to be used for a different purpose by Kaldor in his "model of the trade cycle" (Kaldor, 1940, 1960), that the curve representing investment decisions is $S$-shaped. The reason he gives for it is essentially that greater reliance is placed on short-term expectations when the economy is close to its equilibrium rate of accumulation than when it is farther away from it:

For when things are improving entrepreneurs become more optimistic about their future, and the rate of investment decisions increases strongly; but after a certain point doubts begin to arise as to the stability of this development, optimism ceases to keep pace with the boom, and the rate of investment decisions tends to increase less rapidly. In the slump a symmetrical development is likely to occur. (Kalecki, 1939, p. 135)

For Kalecki the point was that, whereas it is difficult to believe that $|I_x - S_x|$ is everywhere small, it may well be quite small near the equilibrium.

If $|I_x(x^*) - S_x(x^*, v^*)|$ is small enough a single shock will be enough to produce oscillations of slowly diminishing amplitude,

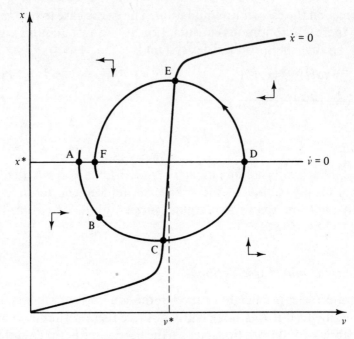

**Figure 7.1**

"slightly damped fluctuations", and a series of shocks "establishes a state of relatively regular undamped fluctuations" (Kalecki, 1939, p. 148, footnote).

To tell the story of these cycles it is helpful to supplement the verbal description with a phase portrait. Figure 7.1 is a phase diagram in the positive quadrant of the $(v,x)$-plane. The horizontal line is the locus along which $\dot{v}=0$ in (7.3), the solution to the equation $I(x^*)=n$. Since $I_x$ is positive, trajectories are traveling westwards above it and eastwards below it. In the first case there is overinvestment $(I > n)$ and in the second case there is underinvestment $(I < n)$.

The locus along which $\dot{x}=0$ in (7.13) satisfies the equation $I(x)=S(x, v)$, which is assumed to define $v$ as an implicit function of $x$ for all positive $x$. It is also the locus along which net windfalls are zero. Its gradient is

$$\frac{\mathrm{d}v}{\mathrm{d}x}=(I_x-S_x)/S_v. \tag{7.20}$$

The trajectories are traveling northwards to the right of it and southwards to the left of it. For since $Q_v^* = -S_v$ is positive, net windfalls are positive ($I > S$) to the right and negative ($I < S$) to the left, and $\partial(\dot{x}/x)/\partial v$ in (7.13) is positive.

In the figure the locus is drawn as a curve which rises steeply as it passed through the equilibrium, in order to be consistent with the assumption appropriate for slightly damped oscillations, namely that $I_x - S_x$ is negative but its absolute value is small near the point $(v^*, x^*)$.

Now suppose, for example, that the initial state of the system is at point B in the figure, where both $x$ and $v$ are below their equilibrium values. This situation could have arisen if, starting from a position of equilibrium, there were a parametric decrease in the inducement to invest. For its effect would be to increase both $x^*$ and $v^*$. The increase in $x^*$ is required to keep the equilibrium rate of accumulation equal to $n$; and the increase in $v^*$ is required because without it planned saving would be greater than $n$ at the higher $x^*$.[1]

In the initial phase the fall in the inducement to invest has created both net windfall losses ($I < S$) and underinvestment ($I < n$) therefore, at B $x$ is falling and $v$ is rising. The employment rate, which increases with $x/v$, is decreasing. For the demand for efficiency labor relative to the supply $x/v = N^d/N^s = xK/N^s$ is an increasing function both of $x$ and of $K/N^s$. But since the marginal propensity to save exceeds the marginal inducement to invest, and since decumulation of capital per unit of efficiency labor decreases saving plans, there are two forces acting to eliminate windfall losses and to halt the decline of $x$ at point C.

In the second phase, starting when $Q^*$ has become zero, $x$ is below $x^*$, so that there is still underinvestment. Hence planned saving continues to decrease, turning aggregate windfall losses into aggregate windfall profits. Consequently $x$ and $v$ are now both rising, the rise in $x$ being due to windfall profits and the rise in $v$ to underinvestment. The recovery of $x$ could, if it were strong enough, draw the economy to its equilibrium in this phase without overshooting. But if $|I_x - S_x|$ is sufficiently small this tendency will be too weak to prevent the upward movement of $x$ from point C to point D in the figure, as aggregate demand is stimulated by the underinvestment brought about when $x$ is low. Thus "we obtain an upward 'self-stimulating' process" (Kalecki, 1939, p. 143) of investment and output on a given capital. When $x$ reaches $x^*$ at point D the ratio of capital to efficiency labor is above its equilibrium value. But before $x$ reaches $x^*$ the downward movement of the employment rate is reversed, as windfall profits increase $x$ and higher $x$ reduces the magnitude of underinvestment, attenuating the depressive effect of decreasing $K/N^s$ on the ratio of the demand for labor to the supply.

The third phase beginning at point D is a reflection of the first, as it were. It has positive net windfalls $(I > S)$ and overinvestment $(I > n)$. Hence $x$ is rising, $v$ is falling, and the employment rate is increasing. But the rise in $x$ and fall in $v$ are both acting to eliminate windfall profits, bringing to a halt the rise in $x$ at point E.

Similarly the fourth phase mirrors the second. It begins with $Q^*$ negative and overinvestment, so that both $x$ and $v$ begin to fall. As in the second phase there is overshooting, because the tendency of falling $x$ to increase $I - S$ is weak in comparison with the opposite tendency of overinvestment to reduce it. There is "a downward 'self-stimulating' process" of investment and output on a given capital (Kalecki, 1939, p. 144), and overinvestment continues until $x$ has fallen to $x^*$ at point F, where the ratio of capital to efficiency labor is below its equilibrium value. Before this, however, the employment rate has reached its peak and started to fall, as windfall losses decrease $x$ and lower $x$ reduces the magnitude of overinvestment. Thereafter the continuance of the fall in $x$ adds underinvestment to aggregate windfall losses. The economy has returned to the phase from which a new cycle begins, except that in the absence of further shocks its amplitude will be smaller.

### Real Wages and Employment

In connection with the long-continuing debate on the question whether real efficiency wages are or are not procyclical in some sense one should mention a distinctive quality of overinvestment theories with a variable employment rate. In the purely monetary theories of chapter 6 the constancy of $v$ implies that the real efficiency wage (measured by $w/p$) is the only factor affecting the employment rate, so that with respect to that rate real efficiency wages are anticyclical except under the extreme assumption of cost-determined prices, in which case they are constant. But in overinvestment theories with a variable employment rate, unless prices are cost-determined, there can be an alternation between pro-cyclical and anticyclical real efficiency wages with respect to it.

An instance of this occurs in the model just presented. For since changes in the employment rate are due not only to changes in $w/p$ but also to changes in $v$ brought about by overinvestment and underinvestment, in the course of a cycle there is a procyclical phase in which the tendency of rising real wages to decrease the rate is overborne by the tendency of overinvestment (rising $K/N^s$) to increase it, and likewise a procyclical phase in which the tendency of falling real wages to increase the rate is overborne by the tendency of underinvestment (falling $K/N^s$) to reduce it. On the trajectory pictured in figure 7.1 these phases begin at points E and C respectively, at which the only influence on the employment rate is the change in $K/N^s$, and terminate when the direction of $x/v$ is reversed.

## Kalecki's Dynamics

In the business cycle described by Kalecki himself (1939, pp. 141–9) there are no windfall profits or losses. Also overinvestment and underinvestment (changes in $v$) affect aggregate demand through their influence on investment decisions. They have no influence on planned saving. Here is a set of assumptions which follow quite closely Kalecki's line of thought and by means of which these features can be depicted.

1  The economy is always in a short-period equilibrium (p. 117).
2  The current rate of accumulation

$$\dot{K}/K = I = S(x) \tag{6.27}$$

has been determined by past decisions (p. 124).
3  There is a justified rate of accumulation $J$ such that the actual rate of accumulation increases or decreases according to whether $J$ is greater or less than $I$:

$$\dot{I} = \epsilon(J - I). \tag{7.21}$$

where $\epsilon$ is a positive coefficient of adjustment. This is a distributed-lag representation in continuous time of Kalecki's postulate that investment decisions influence investment with a constant average lag (p. 126). Compare (5.22) above.

4  Justified accumulation is an increasing function of both $x$ and $v$:

$$J=J(x, v) \tag{7.22}$$

with $J_x$ and $J_v$ both positive.

The second-order system implied by these assumptions is

$$\dot{x}=\psi(x)[J(x, v)-S(x)] \tag{7.23}$$

$$\dot{v}=v[n-S(x)], \tag{7.24}$$

where

$$\psi(x)=\epsilon/S'(x). \tag{6.34}$$

The structure of this system is so much like that of equations (7.13) and (7.3) that a detailed analysis would be tedious. Obviously there will be slightly damped fluctuations if $J_x(x^*, v^*) - S'(x^*)$ is negative and its absolute value is sufficiently small. Figure 7.1 is still relevant for the phase portrait. But now the horizontal line along which $\dot{v}=0$ is the solution to the equation $S(x^*)=n$, and the curve along which $\dot{x}=0$ satisfies the equation $J(x,v)=S(x)$, whose gradient is

$$\frac{dv}{dx}=-[J_x-S'(x)]/J_v. \tag{7.25}$$

Since $S'(x)$ and $J_v$ are positive, the directional arrows must be as before.

If an equilibrium is disturbed by a parametric decrease in justified investment there is no change in $x^*$ but $v^*$ is increased. The increase in $v^*$ is required in order sustain the equation $J(x^*, v^*)=n$. Thus the initial state of the system will be at a point like A in the figure, where $x=x^*$ but $v$ is less than $v^*$.

The fall in justified investment below actual saving investment causes actual investment, and therefore $x$ also, to decrease, leading to underinvestment. Thereafter the successive phases are similar to those of the previous model, the main differences being that $J(x, v)-S(x)$ takes the place of $Q^*$ and $S(x)-n$ takes the place of $I(x)-n$.

Actually in Kalecki's narrative it is not the factor-supply ratio $K/N^s$ but the stock of capital equipment $K$ that has an adverse influence on investment decisions when it increases and a favorable influence when it decreases (1939, p. 144). But to account for this it is only necessary to assume, as he did, that "We are dealing with an economy with no secular trend" (p. 117). If $N^s$ is a constant a change of $v$ is equivalent to a change of $K$ in the opposite direction.

The first version of Kalecki's theory appeared in Polish in 1933. In that version homogeneity of aggregate demand was prevented by autonomous consumption (Kalecki, 1971, Essay 1, p. 1). It is remarkable, therefore, not only for having anticipated Keynes's short-period equilibrium but also for having provided for an extreme Keynesian long-period equilibrium long before the problem of the trend presented itself to Keynes's successors.

### 7.5 Kaldor's Inevitable Cycle

*A Relaxation Oscillation*

Kaldor (1940, and 1960, Essay 8) takes the general system arising from Assumptions (7.1)–(7.3) and the inclusion of autonomous expenditures:

$$Q^* = I(x, v) - S(x, v) \tag{7.9}$$

$$\dot{x} = xaH[Q^*(x, v)] \tag{7.13}$$

$$\dot{v} = v[n - I(x, v)] \tag{7.14}$$

$$I_v \geq 0 \text{ and } S_v \leq 0 \tag{7.11}$$

$$I_v S_v \neq 0, \tag{7.12}$$

and grafts onto it further "assumptions under which the combined operation of the so-called "multiplier" and the investment demand function . . . inevitably gives rise to a cycle" (1960, Essay 8, p. 177).

His choice of conditions gives rise to a relaxation oscillation. Such oscillations are a particular type of periodic motions requiring no shocks to sustain them. Relaxation phenomena arise when a dynamic system is regulated by more than one regime of continuous motion, each of which must terminate after a finite interval, but at the point of termination a rule dictated by non-mathematical considerations imposes a discontinuous switch to another regime of continuous motion. There is a relaxation oscillation if the motions become repetitive. Le Corbeiller (1933) had previously suggested the possibility of explaining business cycles as relaxation oscillations, but Kaldor seems to have been the first to exploit it.

Actually the previous section's simpler version of this system with autonomous consumption but no autonomous investment is quite adequate as a vehicle for Kaldor's theory. Let us therefore endow the model

$$Q^* = I(x) - S(x, v) \tag{7.21}$$

$$\dot{x} = xaH(Q^*) \tag{7.22}$$

$$\dot{v} = v[n - I(x)]. \tag{7.3}$$

with his three basic assumptions.

### Assumption (7.4)

At the point of equilibrium the marginal inducement to invest exceeds the marginal propensity to save (Kaldor, 1960, p. 181), so that the equilibrium is completely unstable.

### Assumption (7.5)

The function $I(x)$ is non-linear (p. 180), as in Kalecki's theory, and in conjunction with the function $S(x, v)$ it is such that $Q_x^* = I_x - S_x$ is negative for every $v$ when $|x - x^*|$ is sufficiently large. Moreover for every $x$ there is a value of $v$ at which $I(x) = S(x, v)$.

### Assumption (7.6)

As in Keynes's *General Theory* the multiplier is instantaneous. For every $v$ the value assumed by $x$ is always such as to put the economy into a short-period equilibrium, that is, such as to make $Q^*(x, v) = 0$, because short-term expectations are always fulfilled. The absolute magnitude of $H(Q^*)$ when $Q^*$ is non-zero is so large that "a position of short-period equilibrium can be reached *before* significant changes occur in the amount of equipment in existence" (Kaldor, 1960, p. 190).

The easiest way of establishing the nature of the cycle implied by these conditions is by recourse to a phase diagram in the $(v, x)$-plane. In figure 7.2 as in figure 7.1, the horizontal line is the solution to the equation $I(x^*)=n$. It is the locus along which $\dot{v}=0$ in (7.3), and $v$ is decreasing or increasing according to whether $x$ is greater or less than $x^*$.

By Assumption (7.5)

$$Q^*=I(x)-S(x, v)=0, \tag{7.23}$$

the locus along which net windfalls are zero, defines $v$ as an implicit function of $x$ for all positive $x$, whose gradient is (7.20). This function, call it $v(x)$, is single-valued. But Assumptions (7.4) and (7.5) imply that the gradient is negative at the equilibrium and positive when $|x-x^*|$ is sufficiently large. Therefore when viewed from the $v$-axis the locus is $S$-shaped, with a backward-rising segment passing through the equilibrium. In other words, regarded as stating the dependence of $x$ on $v$, say $x(v)$, it is multi-valued with three branches: (1) a decreasing function passing through the

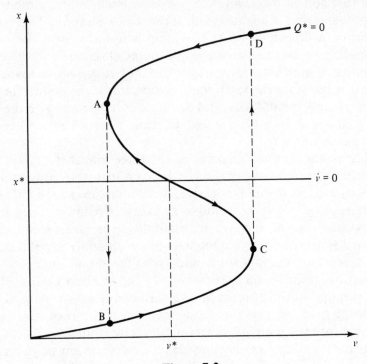

**Figure 7.2**

equilibrium $(x^*, v^*)$; (2) an increasing function emanating from the point marked A in the figure at which $v(x)$ is a minimum; and (3) an increasing function emanating from the origin and terminating at the point marked C in the figure at which $v(x)$ is a maximum.

Since $S_v$ is negative, $Q^*$ and $\dot{x}$ are positive to the right of the ($Q^*=0$)-locus and negative to the left of it. In the absence of Assumption (7.6) $\dot{x}$ would be zero along it. But Assumption (7.6) implies that every continuous motion must satisfy equations (7.23) and (7.3) for as long changes in the value of $v$ regulated by (7.3) permit net windfalls to be kept at zero by continuous movements of $x$. Hence every continuous motion is along the ($Q^*=0$)-locus. The direction of the movements along it is determined by the sign of $\dot{v}$. Mathematically any continuous motion of the dynamic system is regulated by one of the four regimes of the first-order differential equation in $v$:

$$\dot{v}/v = n - I[x(v)]. \tag{7.24}$$

Assumption (7.6) also implies that, whenever at a point $(x, v)$ there are non-zero net windfalls, however small, $x$ must jump from it to a value that eliminates them at the same value of $v$, that is, to a point on a branch of $x(v)$. The jump is upwards or downwards according to whether at the initial point $Q^*(x, v)$ is positive or negative. It must therefore be to one of the two *increasing* branches of $x(v)$. For since the jump must be upwards if the point is to the right of the ($Q^*=0$)-locus, and downwards if the point is to the left of it, it is not possible for the decreasing branch of $x(v)$ to be reached in this way.

The points A and C separating the three branches of $x(v)$ are critical for the behavior of the system. At A there is overinvestment ($I > n$) and therefore $\dot{v}$ is negative. But if $v$ were ever so slightly less than its value at A there would be an excess of planned saving over investment, that is, negative net windfalls, to prevent which $x$ must jump downwards, carrying the state of the economy to point B. At the same time the sign of $\dot{v}$ undergoes an abrupt change from negative to positive; for the downward jump of $x$ is to a value below $x^*$, turning overinvestment into underinvestment. At point C the opposite situation prevails. Underinvestment is turned into over-investment by a jump of $x$ carrying the state from C to D.

By the same logic $x$ must jump downwards from any point on the decreasing branch of $x(v)$ between A and the equilibrium (where $\dot{v}$

is negative), and must jump upwards from any point on it between C and the equilibrium (where $\dot{v}$ is positive). The continuous solutions of (7.24) along this branch fall outside the scope of the system.

It follows that, unless by an extraordinary chance the economy is initially at its unstable equilibrium, it will reach, after at most one non-periodic oscillation, a periodic motion consisting of a jump from A to B, a continuous motion from B to C, a jump from C to D, and a continuous motion from D to A. A "crisis" due to negative net windfalls is induced by overinvestment at point A. This sends the economy into a slump: a low-level short-period equilibrium at B with underinvestment. The movement from B to C is the recovery, in that during this phase there is a tendency for net windfall profits to emerge, as underinvestment reduces planned saving. But their magnitude is insignificant until underinvestment has brought the economy to C. At this point the positive net windfalls induced by underinvestment turn the revival into a boom, carrying the economy to a high-level short-period equilibrium at D

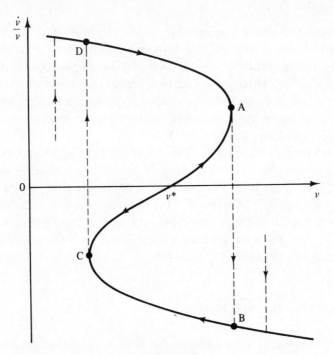

**Figure 7.3**

with overinvestment. In the last phase the boom is progressively undermined as overinvestment, by increasing planned saving, creates a tendency for the emergence of net windfall losses and leads to a repetition of the crisis at A.

There is a close correspondence between Kaldor's economic cycle and a vacuum-tube oscillation analysed by Andronov and Chaikin (1949, ch. IV, pp. 171–4). This becomes evident when a phase portrait of (7.24) is drawn in the right half of the $(v, \dot{v}/v)$-plane. In figure 7.3, which should be compared with their figure 167 (p. 173), the curve through the equilibrium point $(v^*, 0)$ is the multi-valued function $n - I[x(v)]$ and the directional arrows marked on it are self-explanatory. The points A, B, C, and D have respectively the same significance as the points marked with these letters in figure 7.2. The dotted arrows show discontinuous changes of $\dot{v}$. The perpetual cycle consists of a jump from A to B, a continuous phase from B to C, a jump from C to D, a continuous phase from D to A, and so on indefinitely.

*A Historical Note*

An essentially similar relaxation oscillation was later derived by Goodwin, who combined the dynamic multiplier with a "naive" but non-linear accelerator (Goodwin, 1951a, pp. 8–10). He did not refer to Kaldor's theory – a fact that is probably to be explained by Kaldor's failure to include the crucial Assumption (7.6) in his text; it is tucked away in the passage which we have quoted from the Appendix (Kaldor, 1960, p. 190).

Indeed in the text itself (p. 183, footnote 2) he appeared to claim that there must be a stable limit cycle even if the multiplier process is not very rapid. But in response to a challenge some thirty years later by Chang and Smyth (1971) concerning the sufficiency of his conditions for this result he admitted that the theory presented in his paper was founded on the instantaneous multiplier assumed in the Appendix (Kaldor, 1971, p. 46).

### 7.6 The Hicks–Goodwin Contribution

A relaxation oscillation without Assumption (7.6) can be made to emerge from the autonomous-investment model

$$Q^* = I(x, v) - S(x) \qquad\qquad (7.25)$$

$$\dot{x} = xaH(Q^*) \qquad\qquad (7.22)$$

$$\dot{v} = v[n - I(x, v)] \qquad\qquad (7.14)$$

under assumptions cognate with those of Hicks (1950) and Goodwin (1951b). The equilibrium is unstable but there are barriers preventing indefinite expansion on the one hand and indefinite contraction on the other. The economy is governed by the above regime so long as it is free to move inside the two barriers, but whenever either constraint is binding it forces a switch to a different regime defined by the nature of the constraint.

## Unstable Equilibrium

We assume that there is a unique long-period equilibrium $(x^*, v^*)$ satisfying (7.16). But reference to equations (7.18) and (7.19) reveals that when $I_v$ is positive the assumption that the marginal inducement to invest exceeds the marginal propensity to save at the equilibrium point is not enough to guarantee that it is unstable. For the term $-v^* I_v$ in the trace is a stabilizing factor. The reason is that, although an upward (or downward) displacement of $v$ from $v^*$ causes $x$ to start rising (or falling), it also causes overinvestment (or underinvestment), tending to draw $v$ back again to $v^*$. This effect could be strong enough to overcome the cumulative movement of $x$ implied by the fact that $I_x(x^*, v^*)$ exceeds $S_x(x^*)$. Hence Assumption (7.4) must yield to:

## Assumption (7.4)'

At the point of equilibrium $x^*aH'(0)(I_x - S_x) - v^* I_v$ is positive, so that the equilibrium is completely unstable.

## The Floor

In the Hicks–Goodwin theory the influence of short-term considerations on investment decisions does not fade during the boom, but it disappears altogether in a sufficiently deep depression. The reason given by both Hicks (pp. 102–4) and Goodwin (p. 449) is that induced gross investment cannot be negative. Apparently part of the capital stock has been created entirely in response to short-term expectations. But this notion is so peculiar that it seems better to suppose, with Kalecki, that the reason is a psychological one. The pessimism of entrepreneurs in bad times is contained by a conviction that things cannot get much worse.

To capture this feature let us substitute for Assumption (7.5):

## Assumption (7.5)'

There is a unique constant $q < x^*$ such that the marginal inducement to invest $I_x(x, v)$ is greater than the marginal propensity to save $S_x$ for all $x > q$ but is zero for all $x < q$. Moreover for every $x \leq q$ there is a value of $v$ at which $I = S(x)$.

We shall show that this assumption can be used to guarantee the existence of a floor from which first $x$ and then the ratio of capital to efficiency labor $1/v$ must begin to rise.

Let $v_1(x)$ be the function defined implicitly by $I(x, v) - S(x) = 0$, the locus along which $\dot{x} = Q^* = 0$. By Assumption (7.5)' it starts from the origin. It has a maximum at $q$. For its derivative

$$v_1'(x) = -(I_x - S_x)/I_v \tag{7.26}$$

changes sign from positive to negative as $x$ increases through $q$. Since $I_v$ is positive $\dot{x}/x = aH[I(x, v) - S(x)]$ in the second-order system is positive or negative according to whether $v$ is greater or less than $v_1(x)$

Similarly let $v_2(x)$ be the function defined implicitly by $n - I(x, v) = 0$, the locus along which $\dot{v} = 0$. It is a decreasing function for all $x \geq q$ but is constant for all $x \leq q$. For its derivative

$$v_2'(x) = -I_x/I_v \tag{7.27}$$

is negative when $x$ exceeds $q$ and is zero when $q$ exceeds $x$. The constant value, which we shall call $v_q$, is the solution to the equation $n - I(q, v) = 0$. Since $I_v$ is positive $\dot{v}/v = n - I(x, v)$ in the second-order system is negative or positive according to whether $v$ is greater or less than $v_2(x)$.

Since $v_1(x)$ increases from the origin to $q$ every trajectory along which $v$ is increasing and $x$ is decreasing must pass through this locus, whereupon $\dot{x}$ becomes positive. Hence underinvestment leads to a lower turning-point for $x$.

There must, however, be trajectories through points at which $x$ is less than $q$ and $v$ equals $v_q$. To establish what happens then we observe that $v_q$ must exceed all values of $v_1(x)$ with $x \leq q$. For since

$$v_2'(x) - v_1'(x) = -S_x/I_v \tag{7.28}$$

exists and is negative except at $q$, the function $v_2(x) - v_1(x)$, which is zero at the equilibrium, increases monotonically as $x$ decreases from $x^*$. Therefore at any point $(x, v_q)$ at which $x$ is no greater than $q$: (1) $v$ is a constant because $I = n$; (2) $x$ must be rising because $v = v_q > v_1(x)$. The first-order regime

$$\dot{x}/x = aH[n - S(x)] > 0 \tag{7.29}$$

$$v = v_q \tag{7.30}$$

must consequently govern the state of the economy until $x$ has risen above $q$. But at that stage $I$ becomes greater than $n$ and $\dot{v}$ becomes negative, so that the subsequent motion must be governed by the second-order system. Thus if in the course of its motion the economy reaches a point at which $I(x, v) = n$ and $x \leq q$, it switches to this regime in which $v$ is constant and $x$ is increasing. But when $x$ has risen above $q$ and consequently $I$ has risen above $n$ the free motion governed by the second-order system will be resumed.

### The Ceiling

Hicks assumes a rigid barrier at "Full Employment" (1950, p. 96) – "a direct restraint upon upward expansion in the form of a scarcity of employable resources" beyond which "it is impossible for output to expand without limit" (p. 95).

There is a difficulty here (noted by Hicks, p. 99, footnote 1) in that the limitation on supply is supposed to place a restraint on aggregate demand. Perhaps the best way round it in our model is to reformulate Assumption (7.2):

### Assumption (7.2)'

Efficiency wages in terms of money are inflexible:

$$F(x/v) = 0 \tag{5.4}$$

whenever $x/v$ is less than a critical constant $\kappa \geq 1$ but (1) they become perfectly flexible upwards whenever $x/v$ equals $\kappa$ and (2) there is not full cost push.

Owing to the non-Keynesian clause (2) changes in money wages will cause less-than-proportional changes in short-term normal prices, and perfectly flexible money wages will entail perfectly flexible real wages, prohibiting the ratio of the demand for labor to the supply from rising above the critical constant $\kappa \geq 1 > x^*/v^*$ at which, by clause (1), efficiency wages in terms of money become perfectly flexible upwards.

Suppose that the state of the economy reaches a point on the ray $x = \kappa v$ at which there is overinvestment, so that $\dot{v}$ is negative, and the free motion implies that $x/v$ is increasing. Then the actual motion must switch to the first-order regime

$$\dot{v}/v = n - I(x, v) < 0 \tag{7.31}$$

$$x = \kappa v \tag{7.32}$$

and remain in it so long as under the regime of free motion $x/v$ would rise above $\kappa$.

But the economy cannot cling to the ceiling indefinitely. When $v$ has fallen below both $v_1(x)$ and $v_2(x)$ net windfall losses imply that under the free motion $\dot{x}$ is negative, and underinvestment implies that $\dot{v}$ is positive. At such a point on the ray the free motion requires $x/v$ to be decreasing. Therefore, there must be a higher point on the ray at which the free motion required it to start doing so. At this point the economy switches back to the second-order regime.

### Oscillations

Figure 7.4 is a phase diagram in the $(v, x)$-plane illustrating how the several parts fit together to form a whole. The loci marked $\dot{x} = 0$ and $\dot{v} = 0$ are the functions $v_1(x)$ and $v_2(x)$ respectively, intersecting at the point of equilibrium. The ordinate of the dotted horizontal line is $q < x^*$, and the abscissa at which this line intersects the $(\dot{v} = 0)$-locus is $v_q$. The ray is the full-employment ceiling. The arrows show the directions of motion under each of the three regimes. At the point labeled A the motion under the second-order regime is due south. Hence a trajectory moving along the ceiling

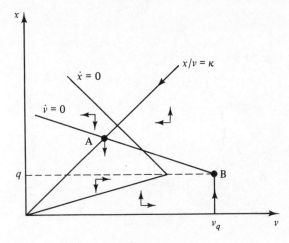

**Figure 7.4**

must leave it above A. Vertically above the point labeled B, the motion under the second-order regime is northwestwards. Hence a trajectory moving due north along the floor must begin to obey the regime of free motion at B.

Starting from any state other than the equilibrium itself the economy will settle after a finite interval into a repetitive oscillation during which it encounters at least one of the two barriers. If the centrifugal forces surrounding the equilibrium are sufficiently strong both barriers will be hit. This case is portrayed in figure 7.5. From B the economy enters a phase in which $x$ is raised by an excess of investment over planned saving (net windfall profits), $v$ is reduced by overinvestment, and $x/v$ is rising towards $\kappa$. At C it bumps against the ceiling and begins to creep along it. But as $x$ and $v$ fall net windfall losses and reduced overinvestment bring about a reduction of $x/v$ below $\kappa$ starting at D. After the ensuing phase of net windfall losses and underinvestment a recovery of $x$ begins at E, because entrepreneurs cease to reduce investment in response to short-term expectations and the increase in $v$ due to underinvestment stimulates aggregate demand enough to raise investment above planned saving. But the centrifugal forces are too strong ($I_v$ is too small) to permit the elimination of underinvestment until $v_q$ is reached. Thereafter $x$ rises with $v$ constant at $v_q$ until B has been reached again, and the same oscillation recommences.

But in relation to the strength of the centrifugal forces the ceiling

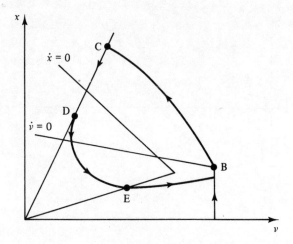

**Figure 7.5**

may be too high for its constraint to be operative (Hicks, 1950, pp. 106–7). The oscillation then has "booms which die of their own accord" instead of "booms which are killed by hitting the ceiling" (p. 107). This case is illustrated in figure 7.6. Along the trajectory emanating from B, overinvestment converts windfall profits into windfall losses below the ceiling, and the consequent fall in $x$ is rapid enough in comparison with the fall in $v$ to bring $x/v$ to a maximum less than $\kappa$. The rest of the story, however, must be qualitatively the same as in the first case. For the centrifugal forces

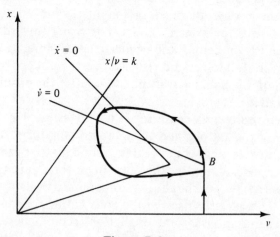

**Figure 7.6**

must still prevent the elimination of underinvestment before $v_q$ is reached; otherwise the trajectory through B would tend to the equilibrium. Thus the repeated oscillation is the trajectory emanating from B and returning to it after an encounter with $v_g$.

Lastly there is the case illustrated in figure 7.7, where the economy hits the ceiling but not the floor. If the centrifugal forces are sufficiently weak ($I_v$ is sufficiently large) the curb on the influence of short-term expectations and the stimulus of under-investment to aggregate demand will raise investment above planned saving before $v_q$ is reached. The oscillation is fixed by the point D at which the trajectory is about to leave the ceiling, the point F at which underinvestment is turned into overinvestment while $v$ is less than $v_q$, and the point C at which the ceiling is hit. Attention to this possibility, not mentioned by Hicks, was drawn by Kaldor in his review article (Kaldor, 1960, Essay 9, p. 196), footnote 3).

## Trend and Cycle

Since our model does not confirm the impression given by Hicks (1950, pp. 104–5) that the upturn requires autonomous investment to be growing, the question arises whether his own model confirms it. As a matter of fact it does, for he assumes (p. 102) that the wastage of the stock of capital due to past induced investment is a

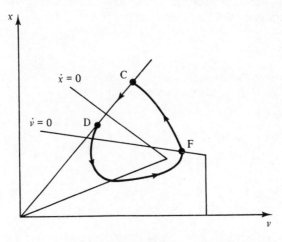

**Figure 7.7**

constant quantity. When the accelerator (which is a determinant of induced investment in Hicks's model) is put out of action by the fact that induced gross investment has fallen to zero, total net investment equals autonomous investment minus a negative constant. Therefore net investment will rise only if autonomous investment is increasing.

Nevertheless the conclusion is obviously not robust with respect to the form taken by the wastage function. If, for example, the stock of capital $K^i$ due to past induced investment deteriorates at a constant proportional rate $\delta > 0$ total net investment is

$$\dot{K} = -\delta K^i + \dot{K}^a. \tag{7.33}$$

where $\dot{K}^a$ is autonomous investment. Then, even if autonomous investment is constant, the shrinkage of

$$K^i = (a \text{ constant}) \times e^{-\delta t} \tag{7.34}$$

causes total net investment $\dot{K}$ to rise. The resulting increase of output via the multiplier brings the accelerator back into action. Presumably this was what Kaldor had in mind when he said that Hicks's presentation is misleading:

The essential link between trend and cycle in Mr. Hicks' presentation consists in his making the growth of autonomous investment responsible for the recovery from a slump. But in terms of the mechanics of his own model this is not necessary. Since induced (gross) investment cannot fall below zero, output cannot fall below a certain minimum, either; when output stops falling, investment must revive, since depreciation exceeds gross investment. (Kaldor, 1960, p. 208, footnote 1)

**Notes**

1   As in chapter 5 let us introduce the shift parameter $\xi$ into the $I$ function with $I_\xi > 0$. Differentiating the equilibrium equations

$$S(x^*, v^*) = n$$

$$I(x^*, \xi) \quad = n$$

with respect to $\xi$ we find that

$$\frac{dx^*}{d\xi} = -I_\xi / I_x < 0,$$

and that

$$\frac{dv^*}{d\xi} = S_x I_\xi / S_v I_x < 0.$$

# 8

# Cycles and Exogenous Growth: the "Classical" Contribution

## 8.1 A Golden Age

Turning from "Keynes" to "the Classics" let us finally consider theories of motion in relation to a *golden age* (Robinson, 1963, pp. 52–3), defined as a long-period equilibrium of exogenous growth in which rates of interest secure the equality of planned saving and investment, wages clear the labor market, and inflationary expectations are realized. Models for such theories can be obtained within our general framework by provided that, when the open-ended dynamic system

$$\dot{x}/x = aH[Q^*(x, m, \lambda)] - bF(x/v) \tag{3.40}$$

$$\dot{v}/v = n - I^*(x, m, \lambda) \tag{3.39}$$

$$\dot{p}/p - \lambda = cH[Q^*(x, m, \lambda)] + gF(x/v) \tag{3.41}$$

has been closed by postulates for the behavior of $m$ and $\lambda$, among the solutions will be a steady state $(x^*, v^*, m^*, \lambda^*)$ satisfying the golden-age conditions

$$I(0, r^*; x^*) = S(0, r^*; x^*) \tag{8.1}$$

$$S(0, r^*; x^*) = n \tag{8.2}$$

$$x^* = v^* \tag{8.3}$$

$$L(0, r^*; x^*, \lambda^*) = m^* \tag{8.4}$$

with $r^*$ and $x^*$ unique and positive.

If the economy is always in a "Tobin–Solow" temporary equilibrium

$$I^* = Q^* + S(Q^*, r^*; x) \tag{1.24}$$

$$\alpha Q^* = \gamma[m - L(Q^*, r^*; x, \lambda)] \tag{3.2}$$

$$r^* = f(x) - xf'(x). \tag{1.28}$$

the equations for a golden age are (8.2), (8.3), (8.4) and

$$I^* = S(0, r^*; x^*) \tag{8.5}$$

$$r^* = f(x^*) - x^* f'(x^*). \tag{8.6}$$

### 8.2 A "Mitchellian" Theory of the Employment Cycle

Distinctive among pre-Keynesian overinvestment theories is the self-generating cycle described by Mitchell (1913, Part III, 1959) in these terms:

1 Prosperity is cumulative. Prices rise in relation to production costs, including wage costs (pp. 16–18), and profits increase (pp. 20–1). At the same time investment is also increased (pp. 23–5).
2 But prosperity breeds crisis, through the "slow but sure increase in the costs of doing business" (p. 29). In particular wages rise and less efficient labor must be brought into employment (pp. 31–5). There is an encroachment of costs on profits (pp. 52–4).
3 Although high rates of interest and monetary stringency may play their part, the failure of prices to rise enough to prevent the encroachment is not primarily due to a shortage of money (p. 54): "Why cannot businessmen defend their profit margins against the threatened encroachments of costs by marking up their selling prices? . . . The only rejoinder that lies upon the surface is that the advance in the price level would ultimately be checked by the inadequacy of the quantity of money . . . But other causes check the rise of price before the banks allow themselves to be jeopardized in this fashion."
4 Among these causes is an excessively high stock of capital:

[W]hen new industrial equipment is placed in active service both the demand for labor, materials, etc., and the current supply of products are enlarged. Hence the encroachments of costs and the difficulty of advancing selling prices are both aggravated. The resulting strain grows progressively more severe so long as prosperity continues to stimulate investment in new equipment . . . The provision of industrial equipment proves inadequate to meet the demand that exists at profitable prices in some branches of trade, and more than adequate in other branches. The whole tenor of prosperity, however, is in the direction of augmenting errors of the latter kind. (p. 57)

5 There follows a phase of cumulative depression (ch. 4, section I.2) during which prices fall in relation to costs, including wage costs (p. 135).
6 But eventually the depression itself breeds new prosperity. For the shrinkage of orders that depression brings and the accompanying decline in selling prices encourages a downward readjustment of costs, and in particular of efficiency wages (p. 139).

## The Model

This is admittedly a narrative in search of a model to justify it: "the self-generating theory of business cycles, which was the hall-mark of Mitchell's ideas on the subject, remained and still remains to be written" (Moore, 1987, vol. 3, p. 482). But it is not difficult to construct such a model. Indeed within the framework of our general system perhaps the nearest approach to Mitchell's line of thought is by way of the present author's model for a non-linear employment cycle (Rose, 1967), or rather by way of a revised version of it based on the following assumptions.

## Assumption (8.1)

Expectations of inflation are constant:

$$\lambda = \bar{\lambda}, \tag{8.8}$$

provided that they are realized on the average, that is, in the long-period equilibrium.

## Assumption (8.2)

Monetary policy is to keep fixed the supply of real balances, but at the level required for a golden age when $\lambda = \bar{\lambda}$:

$$m = m^* = L(0, r^*; x^*, \bar{\lambda}), \tag{8.9}$$

where $r^*$ and $x^*$ solve (8.1) and (8.2), or (8.6) and (8.2).

*Assumption (8.3)*

The derivative $I_x^*(x, m, \lambda)$ is strictly positive.

*Assumption (8.4)*

Efficiency wages in terms of money are nowhere completely inflexible. Moreover they tend to become perfectly flexible upwards when the ratio of the demand for labor to the supply is sufficiently high, and perfectly flexible downwards when the ratio is sufficiently low. More precisely, $F(1)=0$ and there are positive constants $\kappa$ and $\omega(\kappa > 1 > \omega)$ such that $F(x/v)$ is strictly increasing on the interval $(\omega, \kappa)$ and tends asymptotically to $+\infty$ as $x/v$ tends to $\kappa$ and to $-\infty$ as $x/v$ tends to $\omega$.

*Assumption (8.5)*

Both the cost-push coefficient $\sigma$ and the wage-indexation coefficient $\tau$ are less than unity. Consequently both $a$ and $b$ are positive.

*Assumption (8.6)*

The long-period equilibrium is unambiguously unstable.

Putting $\lambda=\bar{\lambda}$ and $m=m^*$ into (3.39) and (3.40) we obtain under these conditions a second-order system

$$\dot{x}=x\{aH[Q^*(x, m^*, \bar{\lambda})]-bF(x/v)\} \tag{8.10}$$

$$\dot{v}=v[n-I^*(x, m^*, \bar{\lambda})] \tag{8.11}$$

in which variations of activity and employment are due not only to overinvestment $I^*-n$ and aggregate demand $aH(Q^*)$, as in the Keynesian models, but also to changes in wage-costs $bF$.

*Unstable Equilibrium*

There is a unique non-trivial steady state at the golden age with $\lambda^*=\bar{\lambda}$. For if $(x^*, v^*, m^*, \bar{\lambda})$ satisfies the golden-age conditions with $\lambda=\bar{\lambda}$, then $Q^*=F=n-I^*=0$, so that $\dot{x}=\dot{v}=0$; and since by Assumption (8.3) accumulation $I^*(x, m^*, \bar{\lambda})$ is a strictly increasing function of $x$, and by Assumptions (8.4) and (8.5) $bF(x^*/v)$ is a strictly decreasing function of $v$, there is no other $x$ at which $\dot{v}=0$ and no other $v$ at which both $x=x^*$ and $\dot{x}=0$.

From the coefficient-matrix

$$\mathbf{K}=\begin{bmatrix} x^*aH'(0)Q_x^* - bF'(1) & bF'(1) \\ -x^*I_x^* & 0 \end{bmatrix} \qquad (8.12)$$

with

$$\operatorname{tr}\mathbf{K} = x^*aH'(0)Q_x^* - bF'(1) \qquad (8.13)$$

$$\det\mathbf{K} = x^*I_x^* bF'(1) \qquad (8.14)$$

we see that by virtue of Assumptions (8.3), (8.4), and (8.5) the determinant must be positive. The equilibrium is therefore not a saddle point. It is asymptotically stable if the trace

$$x^*aH'(0)Q_x^*(x^*, m^*, \bar{\lambda}) - bF'(1) \qquad (8.15)$$

is negative and unstable if it is positive.

We shall stipulate that it is positive in order to implement Assumption (8.6). A small displacement of $x$ above (or below) $x^*$ causes aggregate windfall profits (or losses) of sufficient magnitude to overcome its stabilizing effect on efficiency wages.

### A Stable Limit Cycle

Suppose that the initial state of the system is away from the equilibrium at a point where $x$ and $v$ are positive and $\omega < x/v < \kappa$. Then by the Poincaré-Bendixson Theorem (Coddington and Levinson, ch. 16, Theorem 2.1) the motion from that point must either itself be periodic or must approach a periodic orbit, a limit cycle, as time passes.

*Proof* By Assumption (8.6) the solution through the point cannot go to the equilibrium as time increases. Nor can it carry both $x$ and $v$ either to zero or to $+\infty$; for by Assumption (8.3) $\dot{v}$ is positive when $x$ is less than $x^*$ and negative when $x$ is greater than $x^*$. Lastly by Assumptions (8.4) and (8.5) it cannot reach or tend to the ray $x/v=\omega$, nor to the ray $x/v=\kappa$. For as $x/v$ approaches $\omega$ (or $\kappa$) while $x$ remains finite and positive, $\dot{v}$ will remain finite but $\dot{x}$ will tend to $+\infty$ (or $-\infty$), so that if the solution comes close to either of the rays it will be deflected back into the open region between them. Therefore the three conditions requisite for the Poincaré–Bendixson Theorem are fulfilled: (1) the solution can be continued for all positive $t$; (2) it does not tend to an equilibrium; and (3) it is contained in a closed subset of the open region from which it starts.

∎

Thus if there is only one periodic solution, as it is not unreasonable to suppose, it must be a stable limit cycle. This is the case illustrated in figure 8.1, which is a phase diagram in the positive quadrant of the $(v, x)$-plane. The trajectories must all lie in the interior of the conical region between the rays $x=\omega v$ and $x=\kappa v$ (marked $\omega$ and $\kappa$ respectively) and must wind onto the limit cycle, becoming arbitrarily close to it after a sufficient lapse of time.

The directional arrows are found in the usual way. The horizontal line at $x=x^*$ is the locus along which $\dot{v}=0$ in equation (8.11). Since $I_x^*$ is positive the trajectories are moving westwards or eastwards according to whether there is overinvestment $(x > x^*)$ or underinvestment $(x < x^*)$.

The $S$-shaped curve is the locus $aH[Q^*(x, m^*, \bar{\lambda})]=bF(x/v)$ along which $\dot{x}=0$ in equation (8.10). It defines $v$ as a single-valued function of $x$ for all positive $x$. For by Assumptions (8.4)

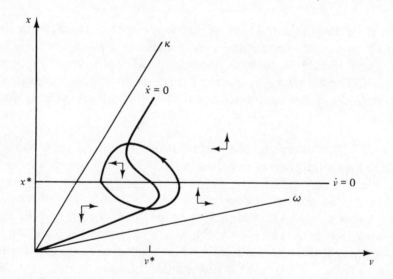

**Figure 8.1**

and (8.5) $bF$ is a strictly decreasing function of $v$ for each $x$ and assumes all real values as $v$ increases in the interval $(x/\kappa, x/\omega)$. Along the locus $x$ must go to zero as $v$ does, and likewise to infinity as $v$ does, in order to avoid contact with the boundaries. In between, however, there must be a backward-rising portion viewed from the $v$-axis. For at the unstable equilibrium its gradient

$$\frac{dv}{dx}\Big|_{\dot{x}=0} = -\frac{x^*aH'(0)Q_x^* - bF'(1)}{bF'(1)} \tag{8.16}$$

must be negative.

Trajectories through points to the right of this locus are moving northwards, and trajectories through points to the left of it are moving southwards. For to the right (left) $v$ is such as to put $bF$ below (above) $aH$ for all $x$, causing efficiency wages to fall (rise) in relation to short-term normal prices.

*The Cycle in Outline*

The Mitchellian phases can be discerned as the economy moves along the limit cycle. The revival of activity $x$ and profits begins when underinvestment has so reduced employment $x/v$ that downward flexibility of wages $w$ is enough to overcome the depressive force of net windfall losses on prices $p$. As the revival proceeds, windfall losses decline and wages become less flexible as employment rises, so much so that revival must lead not to the long-period equilibrium but to a phase of prosperity with high and rising profits and investment.

Prosperity is cumulative at first; for net windfall profits stimulate prices while wage-flexibility remains low. But gradually overinvestment raises employment until wages become so flexible upwards that costs encroach on profits and profits begin to fall.

The course of events from the downturn of activity to its trough duplicates in reverse the course of events from the revival of activity to its peak. The decline of windfall profits as activity falls and the reduced flexibility of wages as employment falls are such as to prohibit an approach to the equilibrium. The downturn becomes a cumulative depression from which, however, the economy is rescued by receding costs when underinvestment has sufficiently reduced employment.

## 8.3 "Non-monetary" Overinvestment Theories

In his *Theory of Social Economy* Cassel pursues an idea with a long history; namely, that overinvestment booms can be broken by rising costs alone, without any deficiency of aggregate demand (Cassel, 1932, ch. XIX). Though production may turn out to have been excessive, it is not essential to the business cycle that it should have done so:

According to a very widely accepted view, the crisis must be regarded as a result of over-production. It would therefore be due to a miscalculation of the demand, an over-estimate of the real needs of the community. We cannot deny that wrong calculations and over-estimates of this sort do commonly play a part in every boom, and intensify the crisis. This was particularly the case with the older forms of crisis. But in modern crisis it is not primarily a question of over-production in this sense. (Cassel, 1932, p. 649)

The primary determinant of cyclical movements is rather the lagged interaction of investment and costs (pp. 641–2). High investment increases costs, rising costs restrict investment, low investment reduces costs, and so on. Haberler calls this the non-monetary overinvestment theory, and finds in it "the culmination of a very important line of thought that can be traced back to Marx" (Haberler, 1963, p. 72).

### A Model for Cassel's Theory

By closing our open-ended dynamic system with Say's law of markets instead of Assumption (8.2), we arrive at a simple model that can serve as a formal approximation to Cassel's thoughts on the subject (cf. Rose, 1968, section III). Specifically, it captures his idea that such cycles must be damped oscillations in response to supply shocks (Cassel, 1932, pp. 644–6).

When there is a constant natural rate of growth the zero-$Q$ temporary equilibrium

$$I(0, r^*; x) - S(0, r^*; x) = 0 \qquad (3.23)$$

$$m^* = L(0, r^*; x, \lambda), \qquad (3.24)$$

with $\lambda = \bar{\lambda}$ by Assumption (8.1), is moved by the second-order autonomous system

$$\dot{x} = -xbF(x/v) \tag{8.17}$$

$$\dot{v} = v[n - I^*(x)]. \tag{8.18}$$

where

$$I^*(x) = I[0, r^*(x); x] \tag{3.27}$$

and

$$r^* = r^*(x) \tag{3.25}$$

is given implicitly by (3.23).

In place of Assumption (8.3) above we need

*Assumption (8.3)'*

The derivative

$$I_x^* = I_r r_x^* + I_x = \frac{I_x S_r - I_r S_x}{(S_r - I_r)} \tag{3.28}$$

is strictly positive.

In Cassel the dependence of saving, the supply of capital disposal, on the rate of interest is not very pronounced "within the limits of ordinary fluctuations in the rate" (p. 245). If $S_r$ is zero $I_x^*$ is equal to $S_x$. And the reason why $S_x$ is positive is that the proportion of entrepreneurs' savings to profits "usually largely exceeds the savings from other groups of income" (p. 620).

To complete the model we retain Assumption (8.4) and replace Assumption (8.5) with the weaker

*Assumption (8.5)'*

The cost-push coefficient $\sigma$ is less than unity. Consequently

$$b = \phi(x)(1-\sigma)/(1-\sigma\tau) \tag{8.19}$$

in (3.43) is strictly positive.

In this system the long-period equilibrium – the golden age of the previous model – attracts all the trajectories that begin in the region where $x$ and $v$ are positive and $\omega < x/v < \kappa$.

*Proof* (1) Since the relevant coefficient matrix is simply **K** above with $Q_x = 0$, its trace is $-bF'(1) < 0$ and its determinant is

$bF'(1)x^*I_x^* > 0$. The equilibrium is therefore locally asymptotically stable. (2) As in the previous case and for the same reasons, every such trajectory is contained in a closed subset of this region. (3) Apart from the equilibrium itself there is no periodic solution. For (a) there is an auxiliary system:

$$\dot{x} = -F(x/v)/v \tag{8.20}$$

$$\dot{v} = [n - I^*(x)]/bx, \tag{8.21}$$

obtained by dividing the right-hand side of (8.17)–(8.18) by the positive function $bxv$, which has $\partial\dot{x}/\partial x + \partial\dot{v}/\partial v = -F'(x/v)/v^2$ fixed in sign everywhere, so that, by Bendixson's negative criterion, none of its regular trajectories can be periodic – none of its integral curves can be closed; and (b) the original system has the same family of integral curves, namely the solutions to the differential equation:

$$v[n - I^*(x)]dx + xbF(x/v)dv = 0. \tag{8.22}$$
∎

The discriminant of **K** when $Q_x$ is zero is $bF'(1)[bF'(1) - 4x^*I_x]$. Therefore the trajectories will spiral towards the equilibrium if

$$0 < bF'(1) < 4x^*I_x. \tag{8.23}$$

After a supply shock the employment rate $(x/v)$ swings to and fro with gradually diminishing amplitude if the effect of real wages on

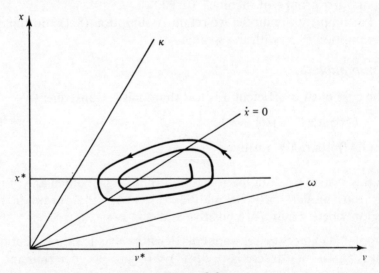

**Figure 8.2**

it $[bF'(1)]$ is small enough in relation to the effect of overinvestment $(x^*I_x)$. This will be the case if wages are sufficiently sticky in some neighborhood of the equilibrium. Other things being equal, the tendency towards oscillations becomes stronger as the centripetal forces represented by $bF'$ become weaker.

The phase diagram is just like figure 8.1, except that the locus along which $\dot{x}$ is zero, and to the right and left of which it is positive and negative respectively, is now the ray $x=v$. The cyclical case is illustrated in figure 8.2.

### Goodwin's "Marxian" Model

In view of (8.19) and (8.23) there must also be oscillations if the elasticity of the demand for labor with respect to real efficiency wages

$$\varphi(x) = -f'(x)/xf''(x) \tag{3.36}$$

is sufficiently small near the equilibrium, provided that the marginal effect of real efficiency wages on the rate of accumulation

$$\frac{dI^*}{dw/p} = I_x^* \frac{dx}{dw/p} = I_x^* \phi(x) \tag{8.24}$$

is not reduced paripassu. The stabilizing force exerted by wage flexibility on employment becomes too weak to prevent the action and reaction of investment and costs.

This observation provides the connecting link between our "neoclassical" model and the original formal treatment of real overinvestment cycles – the "Marxian" model set up by Goodwin in *A Growth Cycle* (Goodwin, 1967). Take the extreme case where there is no substitutability at all between aggregate capital and labor, and suppose that labor's efficiency rises at a constant percentage rate. Then both $Y/K$ and $x$ will be technologically determined parameters within the range of real efficiency wages

$$u = w/p \tag{8.25}$$

that permit a positive short-term rate of profit $Y/K - ux$. Under Cassel's assumption that $S$ is a decreasing function of $u$ only, the temporary equilibrium

$$I(0, r^*; u) = S(u) \tag{8.26}$$

$$m^* = L(0, r^*; u, \lambda) \tag{8.27}$$

is governed by the equations:

$$\dot{u}/u=(c-g)F(x/v) \tag{8.28}$$

$$\dot{v}/v=n-S(u), \tag{8.29}$$

where $c-g=(1-\sigma)/(1-\sigma\tau)$ is positive and $S'(u)$ is negative. Equation (8.28) is obtained by subtracting (3.42) from (3.41) and putting $Q^*$ to zero. When $x$ is a decreasing function of $u$ we have merely an alternative rendering of the neoclassical situation. But when $x$ is a constant $\dot{u}/u$ depends only on $v$ and $\dot{v}/v$ depends only on $u$.

In the latter case, provided that the long-period equilibrium lies in the open region where $Y/K-ux$ is positive and $v$ is between $x/\kappa$ and $x/\omega$, the regular trajectories are the integral curves of the differential equation

$$\mathrm{d}\log T=[n-S(u)]\mathrm{d}\log u-(c-g)F(x/v)\mathrm{d}\log v=0, \tag{8.30}$$

or rather the subset of them that lies in the same region. Since

$$\mathrm{d}^2\log T=-uS'(u)\mathrm{d}\log u^2+(c-g)(x/v)F'(x/v)\mathrm{d}\log v^2 \tag{8.31}$$

is positive, they are the closed contours of a surface $T(u, v)$ that has an extremum at the long-period equilibrium (where $S(u^*)=n$ and $F(x/v^*)=0$). Thus when wages "prey" on capital and employment but not also on wages, every admissible motion of wages ($u$), capital ($1/v$) and employment ($x/v$) is periodic, with an amplitude depending only on the displacement from equilibrium.

This is, I believe, essentially what Marx meant by the contradiction of capitalism and its transitory resolution in booms and slumps . . . The improved profitability carries the seed of its own destruction by engendering a too vigorous expansion of output and employment, thus destroying the reserve army of labor and strengthening labor's bargaining power. This inherent conflict and complementarity of workers and capitalists is typical of symbiosis. (Goodwin, 1967, p. 58)

Goodwin accounts for the Marxian reserve army by having unemployment in excess of unfilled vacancies in the long-period equilibrium. The unique value of $x/v$ at which $F(x/v)$ vanishes is less than unity. The equilibrium is a "limping golden age" (Robinson, 1963, p. 53) with $v^* > x$. There is not enough capital to employ the whole labor force.

## 8.4 Solow's "Contribution": The Neoclassical Ideal

In a frictionless neoclassical environment (1) money wages are perfectly flexible at some ratio ($\kappa$, say) of the demand for labor to the supply, there is no cost push, and factor proportions are continuously variable; (2) investment demand is perfectly elastic at $r=f(x)-xf'(x)$. Therefore (1) money wages are always such that at any given level of expected prices $p$ the expected real wage is

$$w/p=f'(x) \tag{8.32}$$

with

$$x=\kappa v, \tag{8.33}$$

and the dynamic equations are

$$\dot{p}/p=\lambda+H(Q^*) \tag{6.56}$$

$$\dot{v}/v=n-I^*; \tag{8.34}$$

(2) the temporary equilibrium is of the "Tobin–Solow" variety:

$$I^*=Q^*+S(Q^*,r^*;x) \tag{1.24}$$

$$\alpha Q^*=\gamma[m-L(Q^*,r^*;x,\lambda)] \tag{3.2}$$

$$r^*=f(x)-xf'(x). \tag{1.28}$$

This is the scheme behind the neoclassical models of capital deepening developed by Tobin (1955), Solow (1956), and Swan (1956). Indeed with Say's law of markets we have exactly Solow's famous model of neoclassical growth and accumulation under ideal conditions: "[F]ull employment is perpetually maintained" (Solow, p. 67); capital deepening (measured by $-\dot{x}/x=-\dot{v}/v$) equals planned saving per unit of capital minus the natural rate of growth (p. 69); "there is nothing to determine the absolute price level" (p. 79); there are "no monetary complications," (p. 81); and expectations are always fulfilled ("perfect foresight," p. 93). The equations are:

$$\dot{v}/v = \dot{x}/x=n-S[0,f(x)-xf'(x);x] \tag{8.35}$$

$$m^*=L[0,f(x)-xf'(x);x,\lambda) \tag{8.36}$$

$$\pi^*=p \tag{2.3}$$

$$\dot{p}/p=\lambda. \tag{8.37}$$

### 8.5 Tobin's "Monetary" Overinvestment Cycle

In *A Dynamic Aggregative Model* Tobin attributes departures from ideal growth, and in particular cyclical departures from it, to "the inflexibilty of prices, money wages, or the supply of monetary assets" (1955, p. 103), showing how a self-generating monetary overinvestment cycle – a relaxation oscillation – can arise from a non-linear behavior of money wages, an inelastic supply of nominal money, and an unstable long-period equilibrium.

In brief, the story is this. The boom is a period of high employment and of capital deepening. But if the equilibrium of the model is unstable capital deepening must be deflationary; and deflation causes the slump by reducing prices in relation to a wage-floor rigidly fixed in nominal terms. Similarly the slump is a period of low employment, capital enshallowing and inflation; and inflation causes the boom by raising prices in relation to the same money-illusionary level of wages.

Obviously there is a resemblance between this cycle and the Mitchellian cycle of section 8.2 above. But Tobin's argument depends in an essential way on inflexibility of the nominal money supply. And it is really more in the spirit of Keynes than of Mitchell, inasmuch as it also depends in an essential way on the postulate that "labor stipulates (within limits) for a money-wage rather than a real wage" (Keynes, 1936 p. 9).

A much closer resemblance is with the monetary cycle sketched by Hicks in the concluding chapter of *Value and Capital* (1939, ch. XXIV), and elaborated in the concluding chapter of his *Trade Cycle* (1950, ch. XII), where "the monetary factor" is put into relation with the preceding "real theory."

**The Model**

The argument calls for a revision of Assumptions (8.1) through (8.5), the retention of Assumption (8.6), and two extra assumptions.

*Assumption (8.1)'*

Expected inflation $\lambda$ is zero.

### Assumption (8.2)'

Monetary policy is to keep fixed the ratio of (potential) nominal deposits to the supply of efficiency labor:

$$M/N^s = \eta, \text{ a constant.} \tag{8.38}$$

### Assumption (8.3)''

(1) The partial derivatives $Q_m^*$ and $I_m^*$ are positive. (2) an increase in $x$ increases $I^*(x, m)$ if at the same time $m$ changes so as to keep $Q^*(x, m)$ constant:

$$I_x^* - I_m^*(Q_x^*/Q_m^*) = (I_x^* Q_m - I_m^* Q_x^*)/Q_m^* > 0. \tag{8.39}$$

This is the same as saying that the "real" effect of a rise in $x$ on accumulation is to increase it. For in the general case

$$(I_x^* Q_m - I_m^* Q_x^*)/Q_m^* = \frac{I_x S_r - I_r S_x}{(S_r - I_r)}. \tag{8.40}$$

and in the special Tobin–Solow case

$$(I_x^* Q_m^* - I_m^* Q_x^*)/Q_m^* = S_x - S_r x f''(x). \tag{8.41}$$

### Assumption (8.4)'

Efficiency wages in terms of money are perfectly flexible upwards at $x/v = \kappa$ and perfectly flexible downwards at $x/v = \omega < \kappa$. But they are rigid at a *particular* level $\bar{w}$ whenever $x/v$ lies between $\omega$ and $\kappa$.

### Assumption (8.5)''

There is no cost push.

### Assumption (8.6)

The long-period equilibrium is unambiguously unstable.

### Assumption (8.7)

At the long-period equilibrium $w$ is equal to $\bar{w}$ and $x^*/v^*$ is in the open interval $(\omega, \kappa)$.

*Assumption (8.8)*

As in Keynes's *General Theory* (and in Kaldor's trade cycle), short-term expectations are always fulfilled. The absolute magnitude of

$$\dot{p}/p = \lambda + H(Q^*) \tag{6.56}$$

when $Q^*$ is non-zero is so large that for every $v$ the value assumed by $p$ is such as to put the economy into a short-period equilibrium with $Q^*=0$ before any significant change in $v$ can occur.

Actually the function of Assumption (8.8) in Tobin's model is not as vital as it is in Kaldor's. It is rather to provide a neat simplification than to prove the point. For the existence of a relaxation oscillation could be established without it.

There are accordingly three possible first-order regimes of continuous motion. First there is the *sticky-wage regime*. When $x/v$ lies in the open interval between $\omega$ and $\kappa$, $w$ must be equal to $\bar{w}$. Therefore any continuous motion of both $v$ and $\dot{v}$ must be a solution to the system:

$$Q^*(x, m) = 0 \tag{8.42}$$

$$\dot{v}/v = n - I^*(x, m) \tag{8.43}$$

$$m = \eta v f'(x)/\bar{w}. \tag{8.44}$$

Secondly there is the *ceiling regime*. The economy is on the ray $x = \kappa v$ and $w$ is greater than $\bar{w}$. Continuous motion is regulated by the system:

$$Q^*(x, m) = 0 \tag{8.42}$$

$$\dot{x}/x = n - I^*(x, m) \tag{8.45}$$

$$m = \eta x f'(x)/\kappa w \tag{8.46}$$

$$w > \bar{w}. \tag{8.47}$$

Thirdly there is the polar *floor regime*, with continuous motion along the ray $x = \omega v$ The system is:

$$Q^*(x, m) = 0 \tag{8.42}$$

$$\dot{x}/x = n - I^*(x, m) \tag{8.45}$$

$$m = \eta x f'(x)/\omega w \tag{8.48}$$

$$w < \bar{w}. \tag{8.49}$$

## Unstable Equilibrium

By Assumption (8.7) the long-period equilibrium satisfies the equations

$$Q^*(x^*, m^*) = 0 \tag{8.50}$$

$$I^*(x^*, m^*) = n \tag{8.51}$$

$$m^* = \eta v^* f'(x^*)/\bar{w} \tag{8.52}$$

with

$$\omega < x^*/v^* < \kappa. \tag{8.53}$$

Since it is a rest point of the sticky-wage regime, it is asymptotically stable or unstable according to whether

$$\frac{d}{dv}(\dot{v}/v) = \frac{[I_x^* Q_m^* - I_m^* Q_x^*]\eta f'(x)/\bar{w}}{Q_x^* + Q_m^* \eta v f''(x)/\bar{w}} \tag{8.54}$$

is negative or positive at $(x^*, v^*, m^*)$. But the numerator is positive by Assumption (8.3)″. In fulfilment of Assumption (8.6), therefore, the condition

$$Q_x^* + Q_m^* \eta v f''(x)/w = \frac{\partial}{\partial x}\{Q^*[x, \eta v f'(x)/w]\} > 0 \tag{8.55}$$

must be satisfied at $(x^*, v^*, m^*, \bar{w})$. It must, indeed, be satisfied everywhere, to ensure that there is instability of equilibrium whatever the values of $\bar{w}$ and $\eta$ may be.

For the meaning of this condition compare it with (4.15). It is the condition for the instability of a short-period equilibrium if the supply of real balances in terms of wage units ($z = M/wK = \eta v/w$) is constant.

In the special "Tobin–Solow" case, where the temporary equilibrium of $Q$ and $r$ is determined by the equations

$$\alpha Q^* = \gamma[m - L(Q^*, r^*; x, \lambda)] \tag{3.2}$$

$$r^* = f(x) - x f'(x), \tag{1.28}$$

we remember that

$$Q_x^* = [L_r x f''(x) - L_x]\gamma/(\alpha + \gamma L_Q) \tag{3.6}'$$

and

$$Q_m^* = \gamma/(\alpha + \gamma L_Q) > 0. \tag{3.7}'$$

The condition for instability is consequently

$$L_r x f''(x) - L_x + \eta v f''(x)/w > 0. \tag{8.56}$$

Given the money wage, an upward displacement of $x$ entails a higher $p$, because the marginal product of labor is lower. Hence the supply of real balances is reduced $(\partial m/\partial x = \eta v f''(x)/w < 0)$. But the demand for them will also be reduced if the sum of the "income" effect of higher employment $(L_x)$ and the substitution effect of higher interest rates $(-L_r x f''(x))$ is negative. If the demand is reduced more than the supply windfall profits will emerge $(Q_x^* > 0)$, calling for a further increase of $p$ and $x$. (See Tobin, 1955, pp. 109–10, and his Appendix, equation (9).)

## Deflationary Capital Deepening

Under the assumptions of short-period instability and inelastic nominal money, capital deepening along the ceiling must be deflationary (and by a symmetrical argument capital enshallowing along the floor must be inflationary). Accumulation tends to produce windfall losses by decreasing the supply of real balances in relation to the demand for them. Added to this is the tendency of short-period instability to produce windfall losses as $x$ declines pari passu with $v$. When the supply of nominal balances is inelastic ($\eta$ is constant) the supply of real balances will be restored, and the losses avoided, only if there is a deflation of efficiency wages $w$.

For differentiating

$$Q^*(x, m) = 0 \tag{8.42}$$

$$m = \eta x f'(x)/\kappa w \tag{8.46}$$

with respect to $x$ with $\eta$ constant, we find that

$$\frac{dw}{dx} = \{Q_m^* \eta x f'(x)/\kappa w + [Q_x^* + Q_m^* \eta x f''(x)/\kappa w]\} w/m Q_m^*. \tag{8.57}$$

The first term on the right must be positive. But the second term will also be positive if the short-period instability condition

$$Q_x^* + Q_m^* \eta v f''(x)/w > 0 \tag{8.55}$$

is satisfied with $v = x/\kappa$ and $w > \bar{w}$.

*The Cycle*

Figure 8.3 is a phase diagram drawn in the positive quadrant of the $(v, x)$-plane. The downward-sloping curve labeled $\alpha$ is the locus

$$Q^*[x, \eta v f'(x)/\bar{w}] = 0 \tag{8.58}$$

along which net windfalls are zero when $w = \bar{w}$. Its gradient

$$\frac{dv}{dx}\bigg|_{Q^*=0,\, w=\bar{w}} = -\frac{[Q_x^* + Q_m^* \eta v f''(x)/\bar{w}]}{Q_m^* \eta f'(x)/\bar{w}} \tag{8.59}$$

is negative because the equilibrium is unstable. The curve labeled $\beta$ is the locus

$$I^*[x, \eta v f'(x)/\bar{w}] = n \tag{8.60}$$

along which $\dot{v}=0$ when $w=\bar{w}$. It is also downward-sloping and, viewed from the $x$ axis, it is steeper than $\alpha$. For

$$\frac{dv}{dx}\bigg|_{Q^*=0} - \frac{dv}{dx}\bigg|_{\dot{v}=0} = \frac{I_x^* Q_m^* - I_m^* Q_x^*}{I_m^* Q_m^* \eta f'(x)/\bar{w}} \tag{8.61}$$

is positive by Assumption $(8.3)''$. The curves intersect at the long-period equilibrium. The arrows pointing away from the

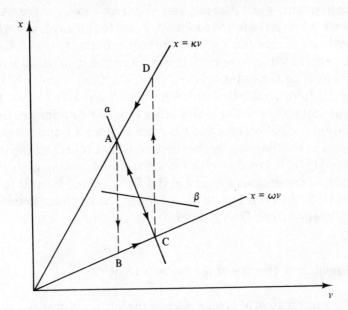

**Figure 8.3**

equilibrium along $\alpha$ show how the system would have to move in the sticky-wage regime. They follow from the fact that, by Assumption (8.3)″ again, $I^*$ is an increasing function of $x$ along $\alpha$.

From any sticky-wage situation off the $\alpha$ curve prices $p$ and employment $x$ must jump upwards or downwards according to whether $x$ is above or below the curve, that is, according to whether the sign of $Q^*[x, \eta v f'(x)/\bar{w}]$ there is positive or negative. For short-period instability entails that this is an increasing function of $x$.

The jump of $x$ is stopped on the ray $x = \kappa v$ (or on the ray $x = \omega v$); for at that point money wages $w$ jump upwards (or downwards) *pari passu* with prices, preventing any further fall (or rise) of the real wage $w/p$. The jump of wages and prices is stopped when real balances have fallen (or risen) to establish a short-period equilibrium at that $x$ and $v$.

Thereafter there is continuous motion of the short-period equilibrium with capital deepening along the ceiling (or capital enshallowing along the floor). For, by Assumption (8.3)″ once more, since $x$ is greater (or less) than $x^*$ and windfalls are zero, $I^*$ is greater (or less) than $n$.

But travel along the ceiling is interrupted at the point marked A in the diagram, where the ray $x = \kappa v$ intersects the $\alpha$ curve. At this juncture wages have fallen to $\bar{w}$ and refuse to fall any lower while $x$ exceeds $\omega v$. Hence the slightest further movement down the ray $x = \kappa v$ causes incipient windfall losses, in response to which $x$ jumps downwards to the point marked B on the floor. Similarly travel along the floor terminates with a jump of $x$ upwards from C to D.

Thus from any starting point other than the equilibrium itself a relaxation oscillation of $x$ and $v$ is reached after a finite interval. It is shown in the diagram by the directed lines connecting the points A through D. It consists of a switch from the ceiling at A to the floor at B, continuous motion in the floor regime from B to C, a switch from the floor at C to the ceiling at D, continuous motion in ceiling regime from D to A, and so on.

## 8.6 Equilibrium Theories of the Business Cycle

. . . the incorporation of cyclical phenomena into the system of economic equilibrium theory, with which they are in apparent contradiction, remains the crucial problem of Trade Cycle theory. (Hayek, 1933, p. 33n)

This passage, quoted with approval by Lucas in "Understanding business cycles" (1981, p. 215), proclaims the program of research on business-cycle theory not only of the Austrian school to which Hayek belonged but also, in our time, of the "new classical" macroeconomists led by Lucas himself. As my concluding topic I take the pair of theories to which this line of research has so far given rise.

## Monetary Malinvestment Cycles

It could be that departures from the aegis of Say's law – from "neutral money" in this sense – are the sole cause of overinvestment cycles. That an untoward injection of new money would start alternating expansions and contractions of capital intensity even though all markets were cleared. And that only in exceptional circumstances is a depression severe enough to create an excess supply of labor. This is the message I glean from Hayek's *Prices and Production* (1935), and more recently from Lucas's "Equilibrium model of the business cycle" (1975).

*The Model*   Let us assume, as we did for the "purely monetary" theory of section 6.2, that $\lambda$ is a constant and that monetary policy is summed up in the equation

$$M/K = \rho e^{\mu t}, \tag{6.8}$$

where $\rho$ is a positive parameter and $\mu = \lambda$. Without significant loss of generality let us also assume that $\mu$ and $\lambda$ are zero. Then under conditions securing perpetual clearing of the labor market we are led, from

$$\dot{m}/m = \mu - \dot{p}/p \tag{6.10}$$

$$\dot{p}/p = \lambda + H(Q^*) \tag{6.56}$$

$$\dot{v}/v = n = I^* \tag{8.34}$$

and

$$x = v, \tag{8.62}$$

to the closed autonomous system

$$\dot{x} = x[n - I^*(x, m)] \tag{8.63}$$

$$\dot{m} = -m\{H[Q^*(x, m)]\} \tag{8.64}$$

regulating the motions of capital intensity ($1/x$ or $K/Y = 1/f(x)$) and real balances when the full-employment temporary equilibrium is displaced from the golden age.

This is almost a specialization of the "synthesis" model in Stein's *Money and Capacity Growth* (1971, ch. 5) with adaptive expectations of inflation. Not quite, however. For in Stein's model the market for final output is not always cleared, and the prices driven by an excess of planned investment over planned saving are assumed to be actual prices, not short-term normal prices.

*Damped Oscillations*   In Hayek's theory high capital intensity brought about by high investment ($I^* > n$) with windfall profits ("forced saving") is likely to be succeeded by low capital intensity brought about by low investment with windfall losses rather than by a monotonic return to the golden age:

Forced saving means essentially a lengthening of the process of production and the crucial point is that, in my view, it is these elongations which are likely to be partly or wholly *reversed* as soon as the cause of the forced saving *disappears* . . . Finally . . . it will appear that, in the case of "forced saving", it is not only impossible to keep the rate of investment constant, but that there will exist, as a necessary consequence of the "forced saving", strong forces which tend to make the rate of investment negative. (Hayek, 1934, pp. 135–6)

It is appropriate, therefore, to seek, from the coefficient matrix

$$\mathbf{L} = \begin{bmatrix} -x^* I_x^* & -x^* I_m^* \\ -m^* H'(0) Q_x^* & -m^* H'(0) Q_m \end{bmatrix} \tag{8.65}$$

with

$$\operatorname{tr} \mathbf{L} = -x^* I_x^* - m^* H'(0) Q_m^* \tag{8.66}$$

$$\det \mathbf{L} = x^* m^* H'(0)(I_x^* Q_m^* - I_m^* Q_x^*), \tag{8.67}$$

for conditions under which the solutions in some neighborhood of the golden age will be damped oscillations.

Let us call upon Assumption (8.3)' of the previous section, whereby $Q_m^*$ and $I_m^*$ and $I_x^* Q_m^* - I_m^* Q_x^*$ are all positive. From (8.66) and (8.67) the first and third of these inequalities are obviously stabilizing. If $Q_m^*$ is positive, a "monetary" displacement from the golden age, consisting of an increase in real balances with capital intensity constant, tends to be self-reversing. By increasing net windfalls it causes short-term normal prices to rise and real balances to fall. If $I_x^* Q_m^* - I_m^* Q_x^*$ is positive a "real" displacement, consisting of an increase in capital intensity with no forced saving (no net windfalls), also tends to be self-reversing. By decreasing the rate of accumulation below the natural rate it causes capital intensity to fall. Thus the equilibrium is asymptotically stable provided that in the trace $-x^* I_x^*$ is less than $m^* H'(0) Q_m^*$.

As we observed in section 3.2, it is quite possible that the partial derivative $I_x^*(x, m, \lambda)$ will be negative, that the positive real effect of an increase in $x$ on accumulation will be overborne by a negative monetary effect. The interesting thing is that this is the circumstance most favorable to damped cycles in the present model.

Indeed, when $-x^* I_x^*$ is equal to $m^* H'(0) Q_m^*$ the eigenvalues of $\mathbf{L}$ are purely imaginary; for at such a point we have tr $\mathbf{L} = 0$ and $D(\mathbf{L}) = (\text{tr } \mathbf{L})^2 - 4 \det \mathbf{L} < 0$. If now $I_x^*$ is increased to a slightly less negative value than this entails, $D(\mathbf{L})$ will remain negative while tr $\mathbf{L}$, which is a decreasing function of $I_x^*$, will become negative, so that the eigenvalues will become complex conjugates with a negative real part.

An initial increase in the stock of nominal money, beyond the demand for it in the golden age, creates a boom of overinvestment and positive net windfall profits; for $I_m^*$ and $Q_m^*$ are positive. Capital intensity starts to rise ($x$ starts to fall) because $I^*$ exceeds $n$. But at the same time real balances start to fall (short-term normal prices start to rise) because $Q^*$ is positive, and in due course tight money leads to turning-points. First it reduces $I^*$ below $n$, so that capital intensity recedes, and then it converts net windfall profits into net windfall losses, so that real balances start to rise. But if $I_x^*$ is sufficiently negative the boom will be succeeded by a slump during which capital intensity falls below the value appropriate to the golden age, and the slump will be succeeded by a new boom after easy money has reintroduced overinvestment and net windfall profits.

The phase portrait in figure 8.4. is constructed so as to illustrate the story we have just told. The ($\dot{x} = 0$)-locus (along which $I^* = n$) is upward-sloping in the $(x, m)$-plane; for its gradient

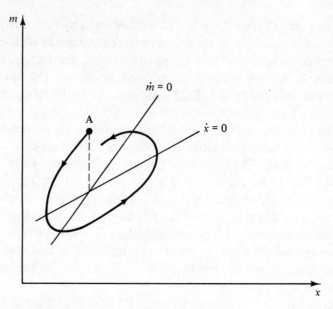

**Figure 8.4**

$$\frac{dm}{dx}\bigg|_{I^*=n} = -I_x^*/I_m^* \tag{8.68}$$

is positive when $I_m^*$ is positive and $I_x^*$ is negative. The $(\dot{m}=0)$-locus (along which $Q^*=0$) is still more upward-sloping; for

$$\frac{dm}{dx}\bigg|_{Q^*=0} - \frac{dm}{dx}\bigg|_{I^*=n} = (I_x^*Q_m^* - I_m^*Q_x^*)/I_m^*Q_m^* \tag{8.69}$$

is positive by Assumption (8.3)′. The representative point moves westwards or eastwards according to whether it is above or below the $(\dot{x}=0)$-locus; for in (8.63) $\partial(\dot{x}/x)/\partial m = I_m^*$ is positive. And it moves southwards or northwards according to whether it is above or below the $(\dot{m}=0)$-locus; for in (8.64) $\partial(\dot{m}/m)/\partial m = -Q_m^*$ is negative.

The trajectory portrayed in the figure shows the course of events described in our narrative, after an increase in nominal money has displaced the system from the golden age (at the intersection of the two loci) to the point marked A.

## The Equilibrium Theory of "Real" Business Cycles

Seven years of abundance came, and the corn was bound in sheaves and taken away to all the storehouses that could be found in Egypt; all that could be spared of the crops was thus stored away in the various cities . . . So the first seven years passed, years of plenty for Egypt; and now, as Joseph had prophesied, seven years of scarcity began; famine reigned all over the world, but everywhere in Egypt there was bread to be had. (*Genesis* 41.47–8; 41.53, Knox translation)

Orthogonal to most other theories is the view that the business cycle is a Good Thing, being no more and no less than the economy's efficient response to exogenous fluctuations in productivity. See Plosser (1989) for an admirably clear exposition of this ingenious idea by one of its originators.

A simple context is a world similar to that of the Solow model, in that the labor force is fully employed and Say's law rules. But (1) the size of the labor force is unchanging and there are no permanent changes in technology; (2) aggregate consumption and investment are as if planned by an everlasting and perfectly well informed Crusoe, maximizing the integral of his instantaneous utilities discounted at a constant rate; and (3) two alternating states of high and low efficiency per worker succeed each other perpetually at equally spaced intervals.

I conjecture, but cannot prove, that in these circumstances the economy will settle down to a cycle with higher consumption and investment in the good times than in the bad times. The argument is as follows.

1  The outcome would probably be such a cycle if no prior notice were taken of the exogenous changes. For in good times Crusoe would be moving optimally towards a stationary state (where consumption equals output and the marginal productivity of capital equals the subjective rate of discount) in which both consumption and capital are higher than they are in the stationary state towards which he would.be moving optimally in bad times.

2  When future exogenous changes are anticipated the amplitude of the consumption cycle will be reduced and that of the investment cycle will be increased; for provision will be made for the bad times in the good times, as it was under the rule of Joseph in Egypt.

The theory becomes more realistic with the introduction of uncertainty and a variable supply of labor. Whether it is to be regarded as the apotheosis of the new classical macroeconomics or as its *reductio ad absurdum* is a question that only posterity can decide.

# References

Andronov, A. A. and Chaikin, C. E. 1949: *Theory of Oscillations*. Princeton: Princeton University Press.

Barro, R. J. 1974: Are government bonds net wealth? *Journal of Political Economy*, 82, 1095–117.

Cagan, P. 1956: The monetary dynamics of hyperinflation. In M. Friedman (ed.), *Studies in the Quantity Theory of Money*, Chicago & London: The University of Chicago Press, 25–117.

Cassel, G. 1923, 1932: *The Theory of Social Economy*, 2 vols, 2nd edn, transl. S. L. Barron. London: Ernest Benn.

Chang, W. W. and Smyth, D. J. 1971: The existence and persistence of cycles in a non-linear model: Kaldor's 1940 model re-examined. *Review of Economic Studies*, 38, 37–44.

Clower, R. W. 1965: The Keynesian counterrevolution: a theoretical appraisal. In F. H. Hahn and F. P. R. Brechling (eds), *The Theory of Interest Rates*, London: Macmillan, 103–25.

Coddington, E. A. and Levinson, N. 1955: *Theory of Ordinary Differential Equations*. New York: McGraw-Hill.

Crick, W. F. 1927: The genesis of bank deposits. *Economica*, 7, 191–202. Reprinted in 1951: A. E. A. *Readings in Monetary Theory*, Homewood, Illinois: Richard D. Irwin, 41–53.

Domar, E. D. 1946: Capital expansion, rate of growth and employment. *Econometrica*, 14, 137–47.

—— 1957: *Essays in the Theory of Economic Growth*. New York: Oxford University Press.

Drazen, A. 1980: Recent developments in macroeconomic disequilibrium theory. *Econometrica*, 48, 283–306.

Duesenberry, J. S. 1958: *Business Cycles and Economic Growth*. New York: McGraw-Hill.

Friedman, M. 1968: The role of monetary policy. *American Economic Review*, 58, 1–17.

Goodwin, R. M. 1951a: The non-linear accelerator and the persistence of business cycles. *Econometrica*, 19, 1–17.

—— 1951b: Econometrics in business-cycle analysis. In A. H. Hansen (ed.), *Business Cycles and National Income*. New York: W. W. Norton ch. 22.

—— 1967: A growth cycle. In C. R. Feinstein (ed.), *Socialism, Capitalism, and Economic Growth*. Cambridge: Cambridge University Press, 54–7.

Haberler, G. 1963: *Prosperity and Depression*, 1st Atheneum edn. New York, Atheneum.

Haltiwanger, J. C. 1987: The natural rate of unemployment. In J. Eatwell, M. Milgate, and P. K. Newman (eds), *The New Palgrave: A Dictionary of Economics*. New York: Stockton Press.

Harrod, R. F. 1948: *Towards a Dynamic Economics*. London: Macmillan.

—— 1952: *Economic Essays*. London: Macmillan.

—— 1973: *Economic Dynamics*. London: Macmillan.

Hawtrey, R. G. 1926 The trade cycle. *De Economist*, 75, 169–85. Reprinted in 1944: A. E. A. *Readings in Business Cycle Theory*. Philadelphia: The Blakiston Company, 330–49.

Hayek, F. A. 1933: *Monetary Theory and the Trade Cycle*. London: Jonathan Cape.

—— 1935: *Prices and Production*, 2nd edn. London: George Routledge & Sons.

Hicks, J. R. 1937: Mr. Keynes and the "classics"; a suggested interpretation. *Econometrica*, 5, 147–59.

—— 1939: *Value and Capital*. Oxford: The Clarendon Press.

—— 1950: *A Contribution to the Theory of the Trade Cycle*. Oxford: The Clarendon Press.

—— 1965: *Capital and Growth*. Oxford: The Clarendon Press.

Joplin, T. 1832: *An Analysis and History of the Currency Question*. London: James Ridgway.

Kaldor, N. 1940: A model of the trade cycle. *Economic Journal*, 50, 78–92.

—— 1960: *Essays on Economic Stability and Growth*. London: Gerald Duckworth.

—— 1971: A comment. *Review of Economic Studies*, 38, 45–6.

Kalecki, M. 1937: A theory of the business cycle. *Review of Economic Studies*, 4, 77–97.

—— 1939: *Essays in the Theory of Economic Fluctuations*. London: George Allen & Unwin.

—— 1971: *Selected Essays on the Dynamics of the Capitalist Economy 1933–1970*. Cambridge: Cambridge University Press.

Keynes, J. M. 1930: *A Treatise on Money*, vol. I. London: Macmillan.

—— 1931: A rejoinder. *Economic Journal*, 41, 412–23.

—— 1936: *The General Theory of Employment Interest and Money*. London: Macmillan.

—— 1973a: D. Moggridge (ed.), *The Collected Writings of John Maynard Keynes*, vol. XIII. London: Macmillan.

—— 1973b: D. Moggridge (ed.), *The Collected Writings of John Maynard Keynes*, vol. XIV. London: Macmillan.

Klein, L. R. 1947: Theories of effective demand and employment. *Journal of Political Economy*, 50, 108–31.

Le Corbeiller, P. 1933: Les systèmes autoentretenus et les oscillations de relaxation. *Econometrica*, 1, 328–32.

Lucas, R. E. 1975: An equilibrium model of the business cycle. *Journal of Political Economy*, 83, 1113–44.

—— 1977: Understanding business cycles. In K. Brunner and A. H. Meltzer (eds), *Stabilization of the Domestic and International Economy*, vol. 5 of Carnegie-

Rochester Series on Public Policy. Amsterdam: North-Holland Publishing Company, 7–29.

Marshall, A. 1920: *Principles of Economics*, 8th edn. London: Macmillan.

Matthews, R. C. O. 1955: The saving function and the problem of trend and cycle. *Review of Economic Studies*, 22, 75–95.

—— 1959: Duesenberry on growth and fluctuations. *Economic Journal*, 69, 749–65.

Metzler, L. A. 1951: Wealth, saving, and the rate of interest. *Journal of Political Economy*, 59, 93–116.

Mill, J. S. 1871: *Principles of Political Economy*, vol. I, 7th edn. University of Toronto Press. London: Routledge & Kegan Paul.

Mitchell, W. C. 1913: *Business Cycles*. Berkeley: University of California Press.

—— 1959: *Business Cycles and their Causes*. Berkeley and Los Angeles: University of California Press.

Moore, G. H. 1987: Mitchell, Wesley Clair (1874–1948). In J. Eatwell, M. Milgate, and P. K. Newman (eds), *The New Palgrave: A Dictionary of Economics*. New York: Stockton Press.

Newcomb, S. 1886: *Principles of Political Economy*. New York: Harper & Brothers.

Nikaidô, H. 1968: *Convex Structures and Economic Theory*. New York: Academic Press.

Ohlin, B. 1937: Some notes on the Stockholm theory of saving and investment. *Economic Journal*, 57, 53–69, 221–240. Reprinted in 1944: A. E. A. *Readings in Business Cycle Theory*. Philadelphia: The Blakiston Company, 87–130.

Patinkin, D. 1948: Price flexibility and full employment. *American Economic Review*, 38, 543–64. Reprinted in 1951: A. E. A. *Readings in Monetary Theory*. Philadelphia: The Blakiston Company, 252–83.

—— 1965: *Money, Interest, and Prices*, 2nd edn. New York: Harper and Row.

Phillips, A. W. 1961: A simple model of employment, money, and prices in a growing economy. *Economica, NS*, 28, 360–70.

Phillips, C. R. 1920: *Bank Credit*. New York: Macmillan.

Pigou, A. C. 1941: *Employment and Equilibrium*. London: Macmillan.

Plosser, C. I. 1989: Understanding real business cycles. *Journal of Economic Perspectives*, Summer, 51–77.

Porter, R. C. 1961: A model of bank portfolio selection. *Yale Economic Essays*. 1, 323–59.

Robertson, D. H. 1928: (First published in 1928 as Theories of banking policy, *Economica*, 8, 131–46.) Reprinted in 1940: *Essays in Monetary Theory*. London: Staples Press.

Robinson, J. 1962: *Essays in the Theory of Economic Growth*. London: Macmillan.

Rose, H. 1967: On the non-linear theory of the employment cycle. *Review of Economic Studies*, 34, 153–73.

—— 1969: Real and monetary factors in the business cycle. *Journal of Money, Credit, and Banking*, 1, 138–52.

—— 1973: Effective demand in the long run. In J. A. Mirrlees, and N. H. Stern (eds), *Models of Economic Growth*. London: Macmillan, 25–47.

—— 1985: A policy rule for "Say's law" in a theory of temporary equilibrium. *Journal of Macroeconomics*, 7, 1-18.

—— 1987: Aggregate demand and supply analysis. In J. Eatwell, M. Milgate, and P. K. Newman (eds), *The New Palgrave: A Dictionary of Economics*. New York: Stockton Press.

Samuelson, P. A. 1939: Interactions between the multiplier analysis and the principle of acceleration. *Review of Economics and Statistics*, 21, 75-8.

Sawyer, M. 1987: Autonomous expenditures. In J. Eatwell, M. Milgate, and P. K. Newman (eds), *The New Palgrave: A Dictionary of Economics*. New York: Stockton Press.

Schumpeter, J. A. 1954: *History of Economic Analysis*. New York: Oxford University Press.

Solow, R. M. 1956: A contribution to the theory of economic growth. *Quarterly Journal of Economics*, 70, 65-94.

Solow, R. M. and Stiglitz, J. E. 1968: Output, employment, and wages in the short run. *Quarterly Journal of Economics*, 82, 537-60.

Stein, J. L. 1971: *Money and Capacity Growth*. New York and London: Columbia University Press.

Swan, T. W. 1956: Economic Growth and Capital Accumulation, *The Economic Record*, 32, 334-61.

Thornton, H. 1939: *An Enquiry into the Nature and Effects of the Paper Credit of Great Britain*. London: George Allen & Unwin. First published in 1802.

Tobin, J. 1947: Money wage rates and employment. In S. E. Harris (ed.), *The New Economics*. New York: Alfred A. Knopf, 572-87.

—— 1955: A dynamic aggregative model. *Journal of Political Economy*, 63, 103-15.

—— 1963: Commercial banks as creators of "money". In D. Carson (ed.), *Banking and Monetary Studies*. Homewood, Illinois: Richard D. Irwin, 408-19.

—— 1969: A general equilibrium approach to monetary theory. *Journal of Money, Credit, and Banking*, 1, 15-29.

—— 1975: Keynesian models of recession and depression. *American Economic Review*, 65, 195-202.

—— 1982: Money and finance in the macroeconomic process. (Nobel Lecture, delivered 8 December 1981.) *Journal of Money, Credit, and Banking*, 14, 171-204.

Wicksell, K. 1934: *Lectures on Political Economy*, transl. E. Classen, vol. II. London: George Routledge & Sons. (First published 1906.)

—— 1936: *Interest and Prices*, transl. R. F. Kahn. London: Macmillan. (First published in 1898.)

Withers, H. 1909: *The Meaning of Money*. London: Smith, Elder & Co.

# Index